Shaped
BY FAITH

Shaped BY FAITH

10 SECRETS TO STRENGTHENING YOUR BODY AND SOUL

THERESA L. ROWE

Guideposts
New York, New York

SHAPED BY FAITH

ISBN-13: 978-0-8249-4764-4

Published by Guideposts
16 East 34th Street
New York, New York 10016
www.guideposts.com

Distributed by Ideals Publications
2636 Elm Hill Pike, Suite 120
Nashville, TN 37214

Guideposts and *Ideals* are registered
trademarks of Guideposts.

Editor: Nicci Jordan Hubert
Cover design: Anderson Design Group
Cover photograph: micahkandrosphotography.com
Interior design and typesetting: Lorie Pagnozzi
Interior photography: David Docimo
Hair and makeup: Melinda Hudson

Library of Congress Cataloging-in-
Publication Data

Rowe, Theresa L.
  Shaped by faith : 10 secrets to
strengthening your body and soul / by
Theresa L. Rowe.
    p. cm.
  ISBN 978-0-8249-4764-4
  1. Women--Health and hygiene. 2.
Women—Life skills guides. 3. Health--
Religious aspects—Christianity. I. Title.
  RA778.R69 2009
  613'.04244—dc22

  2008039470

Printed and bound in the United States of America

10 9 8 7 6 5 4 3 2 1

• • •

OVER THE YEARS, I HAVE TAUGHT MORE THAN A
THOUSAND STUDENTS, AND I WANT TO THANK EACH OF YOU
FOR SHAPING ME INTO THE PERSON I AM TODAY.
THIS BOOK IS DEDICATED TO YOU. MAY GOD BLESS YOU
AS YOUR WHOLE-PERSON WELLNESS JOURNEY CONTINUES,
AND MAY HE BE GLORIFIED IN YOUR LIVES.

• • •

Acknowledgments

First, I thank God for loving me and for allowing me to be used as His instrument. He deserves all the glory.

To my loving and faithful husband, Robin. You always support me in everything that I do. You constantly make me laugh with your dramatic facial expressions. Robin, you are the love of my life, and I adore you.

Much of what I have learned over the years has come as the result of being a mother to seven unique and wonderful children: Christina, Candice, Jeffrey, Hunter, Layla, Ethan and Adrian. All of you inspire me in your own special way. I am blessed to be called your mother. I pray for each of you every day, and I know that God has great and mighty plans for you. Live your lives to please Him, and He will direct your path. I love you with all of my heart.

Susie, I thank you for sharing Jesus Christ with me. You changed my life forever, and I will never cease praising God for your boldness and strong faith.

Thank you, Mom, for giving me the gift of life.

To my best friend, Cindy. I love you and thank you for always opening your heart of wisdom to me.

Thank you, Betty and David, for helping me take care of my children when I was a single parent. I will always deeply appreciate your love and dedication to my family.

To all my friends who challenge me to walk strong and tall before God and men. I want to thank each of you for loving and accepting me for who God created me to be. I love all of you and admire the distinct personality each one of you has. Thank you for being you.

My prayer warrior friends, I thank God for bringing all of you into my path at different seasons in my life. Thank you for being obedient to God.

To my siblings, Donna, Danny and Paul, I love you, and I thank you for accepting me as I am, with all of my faults and flaws.

I especially want to thank Lenore and the Guideposts staff for believing in me as a writer and teacher and for asking me to share my own wellness journey. And, Nicci, you are a doll. Thank you for being patient with me during the writing process. And to Melanie: Thank you for adding the finishing touches on the manuscript. You were an essential teammate.

Contents

A Warm-Up

Why did you pick up this book? I suppose there are many possible reasons. It may have been the bright cover or the interesting title, or because of a resolution you've made to live healthier. Perhaps your current fitness plan leaves you flat everywhere but where it counts. You may be a seasoned fitness aficionado interested in expanding your horizons. Or maybe you've ridden the fluctuating-scale roller coaster, but this time you're scared because you're up a little higher than ever before.

There are plenty of ways to lose weight. Diets and pills abound, personal trainers are available almost anywhere, and gyms have more than enough exercise equipment. The question is this: Is losing weight the most important goal? Of course, it is one goal…if you're like most women who struggle to maintain a figure you're proud of, losing weight often feels necessary. And by following the guidelines set in this book, you will lose weight if your body needs to.

Weight loss, however, is not what this book is about. I have not written a diet book or a quick-fix exercise program, and you will not see any mentions of fitting into those "skinny jeans." And I will certainly not guilt you into starving yourself or forsaking all tasty food. No, *Shaped by Faith* is not about losing weight; it is about creating a synergy of physical and spiritual health. I call it, quite simply, whole-person wellness.

For many women, keeping up a consistent, progressing exercise routine feels near impossible. Life and laziness too often get in the way. The same goes for dieting—after all, can anyone truly commit to calorie counting her whole life?

We need something more, a greater motivation.

I have learned that the greatest motivation for living healthfully is found in my spirit, my connection with God. There is an amazing, often untapped, interconnectedness between our physical and spiritual selves. If we focus on our relationship with God and the spiritual lessons we learn, we can redirect the course of our fitness journeys. In other words, by allowing our spiritual walk to support our physical walk, and by realizing how profoundly our physical growth affects our spiritual growth, we embrace a merging of entities that will lead us closer to whole-person wellness.

I have been a fitness instructor for more than twenty-five years, and I am nationally certified in group exercise, personal training, Pilates, step and interval training. But even still, fitness routines have never been enough to keep me engaged, devoted and growing. Without God as the focus—the point—of my workout routines, I would soon reach my plateau. What's more, as I engage in the constant challenge of maintaining a healthy body, God's spiritual truths take on new, stronger meanings and applications in my life. I have gone through many, many trials, and I know that my ability to overcome them stemmed from both a physical and spiritual core. That is whole-person wellness at its best—our spirits and bodies working together to make us healthier, holier, and more able to endure.

A student of mine who has faithfully attended my strength-training classes for over a year is a perfect example of what it means to pursue whole-person wellness. When she began taking my class, she weighed more than three hundred pounds, and for months, she had to sit in a chair in order to do the routine. But she was determined and attended every session, no matter how little she could actually perform. I could tell she was frustrated and felt weak, and she didn't make much progress over the first few sessions. But after a while, she began to stand during class, and, slowly but surely, her movements became more fluid, beautiful, and her body began to shed some weight.

I was so inspired by this woman that I approached her, curious about what kept her so motivated. She told me that she faced the common health risks of obesity, and that was a factor. But in no uncertain terms, she made it clear to me that her true motivation was in Christ. She explained that she had recently sensed her spirit weakening, and, somehow, she knew that it was because of her weak physique. Since regularly attending the classes, she told me, her spiritual walk had become more vibrant than it had been in years. And her renewed physicality had provided a new sense of gusto in her daily life. Her spiritual strength and dedication to Christ motivated her to do something about her physical body. Today, she continues to attend class. She is still a heavier woman, but she is healthy in body and spirit, and she carries a sweet, confident, content attitude.

Whole-person wellness is not a lofty idea, nor is it new. In Proverbs, a woman who embodies whole-person wellness is described in detail. The Scriptures say, "She rises also while it is still night. . . . She girds herself with strength and makes her arms strong. . . . Strength and dignity are her clothing, and she smiles at the future. . . . She looks well to the ways of her household, and does not eat of the bread of idleness. . . . Charm is deceitful and beauty is vain, but a woman who fears the LORD, she shall be praised" (NASB). Just a quick glance at this passage and we can clearly see the virtues that enable this woman—any woman—to be praiseworthy. She fears the Lord, rejects vanity, yet with holy motivation strengthens her body. Now those are characteristics that make whole-person wellness a journey worth taking.

And it's a journey I want to help you take with *Shaped by Faith*. Each chapter addresses a specific concept central to developing whole-person wellness and is divided into three sections: "Shaped by Life," "Shaped by Fitness" and "Shaped by God."

In "Shaped by Life," I'll tell you a piece of my testimony, because I believe that—whether we see it at the time or not—our life stories are interwoven with our fitness journeys. My life has been wrought with heartbreak, devastation and sickness, yet it has inextricably shaped my wellness journey. I hope that my story not only engages you but also encourages you to apply the lessons you've learned in life to your pursuit of a healthy body.

The "Shaped by Fitness" section will give you practical advice and targeted exercises and workouts to help you incorporate fitness into your daily life. To make the exercises I've written for you as clear as possible, I've taken some pictures to demonstrate the trickier movements I've described. Additionally, at the front of this book, we've attached a twenty-five-minute strengthening and stretching DVD to help get you started on your journey. Even if you are a novice, you will feel right at home with these fitness fundamentals. At the back of the book, in Appendix A, is a sample workout that covers an entire year. This workout is designed to kick-start your fitness journey and provide you with a plan that will help you easily incorporate this book's themes into your life. (Please note that if you have chronic health problems or are pregnant, I'd recommend checking with your doctor before beginning any kind of new exercise program. However, the breathing and posture exercises are beneficial for any and all stages of life, and will be a great foundation for anyone seeking whole-person wellness.)

And because I strongly believe that fitness and wellness are both physical and spiritual, "Shaped by God" will describe how these fitness practices influenced my discovery of God and how my relationship with Him intertwines into my fitness routines. This is where simple fitness actually transcends into whole-person wellness, and I hope the stories, Scriptures, and encouragement here will help you press on toward a higher goal.

At the end of each chapter, I've written a simple prayer, focused on the theme. It may help you to pray these words out loud or write them into your journal. I also hope they will serve as a springboard for many more intimate, personal conversations between you and the Father. May those prayers transcend my own words and become God's blessings on you, spurring you on.

I've also included a "Theresa's Top Three" in every chapter, which will provide you with action steps and thoughts to help you begin to apply the concepts of the chapters.

As you read, remember that whole-person wellness is not a short-term fitness fad, but a life-changing experience that allows us to evolve and mature in both body and spirit. *Shaped by Faith* is loaded with concepts, workouts, and prescriptions, but please don't try to incorporate everything into your life at once. You might want to begin with the Appendix A workout at the back of the book. You also could choose a theme in a chapter that you respond to most, and start there, working your way through the other themes gradually. If you aren't sure which theme you'd like to begin with, the listening chapter is a simple and profound place to start. You might spend two weeks or two months on one theme.

Whole-person wellness is not destination-based, but journey-based, with plenty of roses to smell along the way. The process will be long and will probably unfold over the course of your life. I know I'm still working on it! But with the Spirit as your guide and this book as your tool, your wellness journey will be marked by success, joy and peace.

Once you commit to taking the first step on the road to wellness, write this significant date down. This will not only commemorate your decision, but it will also begin a record of your journey. Journal your fitness challenges and successes, as well as your spiritual mind-set. This will help you to stay motivated and on track, and it will be evidence of the interconnectedness of your soul and body. And many years from now, you'll be able to look back and see how far you and God have come together.

We all know that God answers prayer, so take this journey prayerfully. I am praying for you, too. My prayer is that you will experience the joy that I have discovered in pursuing whole-person wellness. As you go forward, may you live each day with great expectancy and with a faith that energizes your body and soul.

Chapter One

> PAY ATTENTION, MY CHILD, TO WHAT I SAY.
> LISTEN CAREFULLY. DON'T LOSE SIGHT OF MY
> WORDS. LET THEM PENETRATE DEEP WITHIN YOUR
> HEART, FOR THEY BRING LIFE AND RADIANT HEALTH
> TO ANYONE WHO DISCOVERS THEIR MEANING.
>
> PROVERBS 4:20—22

The great American philosopher William James once wrote, "The greatest discovery of any generation is that a human being can alter his life by altering his attitude. As you think, so shall you be." In my years as a fitness instructor, I have found that James's insight is supremely relevant to wellness, and it's a philosophy that I have brought into every exercise class I have taught. After all, without the right attitude, fitness can only take us so far.

An altered attitude means several things. First, it means listening to the voices of our mind, spirit, and especially our body. So many people approach exercise without the faintest idea of what their bodies need. But if you listen, you will see that the body communicates in very specific ways, and if we ignore such cues, we not only risk exercising incorrectly, but we threaten our health altogether. Listening to our bodies is essential to taking the right path toward wellness.

An altered attitude also requires responsive discipline. We must understand that being attentive to our bodies only works if we take action based on what we learn. Let's say, for example, a woman notices that she has trouble keeping a straight posture, which is causing her back pain. Struggling to focus on correcting it, she continues to slouch in defeat. She knows that her chronic back soreness will only get worse, but instead of taking positive action steps, she pops pain medications. This woman is attentive enough to her body to know her problem. But she chooses to perpetuate the issue instead of correcting it with progressive, appropriate changes like stretching, alignment and abdominal strengthening techniques.

Any one of us could be that woman. It's much easier to continue old habits than to create new, healthy ones. But creating healthy habits is what an altered attitude is all about, and it's what this book will require of you. We must listen to our bodies, and we must respond with great care and love for the temple that God gave us.

In fact, paying attention to our physical health is so important that it could even mean the difference between life and death. If I had not listened to my body, I would have died from cardiac arrest.

Shaped by Life

In 1987, I had settled comfortably into my four-year-old role as a fitness and modeling instructor. I was enamored of teaching classes, and seeing consistent results in my students. But during that year my success was overshadowed by a growing health concern. I began to notice that my energy level was gradually, but markedly, decreasing. I tried to reason that my workload and stress were just taking their toll, which made sense. After all, I was trying to run a business, teach modeling, exercise, and raise my two young daughters.

Whatever the reason, it became more and more difficult to teach a simple hour-and-a-half exercise class. I had difficulty breathing, and I was sweating profusely. After a while, I became concerned and decided to visit the emergency room. I explained to the physician that I had shortness of breath and a lack of energy, which was very unusual for me because of how often I exercised. He asked a multitude of questions about my state of mind and concluded that I was just working too much and that my stress load had gotten the best of me. He sent me home and told me to rest a little more.

But the next week, even after taking it easy, I seemed to be getting worse. I was overwhelmed by fatigue, so I made another visit to the emergency room. A different physician saw me that time. He said that I had typical PMS symptoms, and that I simply needed more rest. He told me to stop worrying about my health.

Again and again, I returned to the hospital because I couldn't accept that everything was okay. But each time, a new doctor would listen to my symptoms and dismiss my pleas for tests. One doctor even told me that I just liked attention and that I should see a therapist.

Even though all the doctors were only willing to diagnose me with "PMS-y attention-seeking disorder," I knew my body well enough to be confident that I was not delusional or simply in want of attention.

One evening, I had just completed my last modeling session of the day and was walking out to my car in the parking lot. Even during this relatively mindless action, I had to focus with an aching amount of energy. I was totally exhausted, and the thought of reaching the car for rest was the only thing that kept my feet moving.

I felt like I'd been walking for miles before I finally collapsed in my car, and I tried to mentally prepare myself for what would surely be a cross-country journey home. I drove out of the lot, the white lines on the highway meeting in the middle. The blacktop was waving back and forth.

I sent up a prayer, asking God—whom I knew only as a deity at the time—to help me drive home that night. And I know now that he did. I can offer no other explanation for how I pulled into my driveway, other than God.

Stumbling into the house, I called out to my roommate Cindy. With just a quick glance my way, she rushed to get the thermometer. She took my temperature, which was 103 and climbing. I could hear her speaking to me, but her voice sounded muffled. The room spun and everything appeared distorted, sort of like a Picasso painting. Cindy insisted on another trip to the hospital—surely, she said, *this* would get the doctors' attention. She left my girls with a neighbor and helped me into her car for the twenty-five-minute drive to the hospital's emergency room.

Finally, I was admitted to the hospital. After what felt like hundreds of tests, the doctors were stumped about my condition—but they did know that I was on the verge of cardiac arrest. Without any other options, they decided to test my heart using an echocardiogram.

To their surprise, the test showed signs of congenital heart failure—a hole in my heart. What had appeared to several other doctors as benign stress, PMS, and influenza had actually been a life-threatening syndrome. So after months of testing, heart catheterizations, prescriptions for rest, and more testing, I was scheduled for open-heart surgery.

I felt scared and vindicated all at once. I had listened to my body despite dismissals from professionals, and even though my heart was in trouble, I knew that it was better for the attention I gave it.

It took a long time to recover after the surgery, but I slowly made my way back to being able to enjoy and fully participate in teaching classes. It was a hard road, but I walked away more in tune with my body than I had ever been before.

Shaped by Fitness

Animals seem to have a unique tie to nature—they have even been known to predict or sense sudden natural disasters. When wildlife vacate to another area or gather in a tight group, dogs start howling, horses refuse to enter their barns, cats start running around frantically . . . people take notice. That's because animals' predictions about nature are almost always right. It is similar for humans and our bodies. God has given us a divine biological system to warn us of upcoming physical disaster, and we must pay attention. If I had learned only one thing from my long-awaited congenital heart failure diagnosis, it would be that I knew my body's language better than anyone else—even doctors—and I shouldn't ignore what it was telling me.

Thankfully, I didn't only learn one thing from that experience. I learned many lessons, another of which was choosing the right attitude. I realized that I could either fixate on all the possible negative results or focus on looking ahead to a stronger and healthier heart. After all I had gone through for a diagnosis, it was an easy decision to be excited about my bright future with a healthy heart. I learned how to harness my mind and body to have hope for the future.

Even then I realized my mind and body were inseparable, both of them working together to keep me focused on my body's goal: recovery. But giving the body this kind of careful attention is not only useful in the prevention of serious health problems like heart disease. In our wellness journeys, we must listen to how our bodies respond to even the smallest movements or pangs in order to make the appropriate adjustments, and, thus, maximize our fitness routines and experience the best results. In fitness, this kind of attentiveness is often called mind-body exercise.

Mind-body exercise is not exclusively found in meditation exercise techniques,

> **"In our wellness journeys, we must listen to how our bodies respond to even the smallest movements or pangs in order to make the appropriate adjustments, and, thus, maximize our fitness routines."**

although those genres certainly revolve around the idea. All activities can become mind-body centered simply by a focus on whatever exercise you do. By channeling your thoughts to each movement, breathing with the movement, and paying attention to the way your body feels, you are practicing mindful attentiveness. This is the kind of smart, healthy technique that is guaranteed to improve your workout experience. And when you take this level of awareness to your everyday life, your mental, physical and spiritual elements function in concert to achieve whole-person wellness. I love teaching my students how to connect all three elements while exercising so that they can reap the benefits.

For example, when I teach a strength-training class, I remind my students to start with excellent posture and body alignment before even thinking about lifting weights. I repeatedly remind them to stand with knees slightly bent and body weight evenly distributed as they lift. I talk them through correct breathing patterns. Details are most important while lifting weights, and I expect my students to mindfully lift with purpose and determination. I always notice that my repeat students become keenly aware of their mind-body connection and begin to correct their postures, positioning and breathing without my cues. When this happens, a distinct sense of peace and control settles over the classroom. The students hardly need me anymore—they are connected, mind and body. They are attentive, choosing an attitude of intentionality and optimism.

To get you started, here is one of my favorite exercises for increasing mind-body awareness.

SEATED WARM-UP

Inhale and begin by sitting on your "sits" bones (the bones you feel when you sit up straight on a firm surface) with your legs crossed in front and a lengthened spine. Exhale and pull your naval in toward your spine as you gently press your shoulders down and extend your arms out from your sides. Deeply inhale and slowly lift your arms over your head and look up, toward your hands. Hold this position for several breaths. Exhale and slowly lower your arms back to your sides with your head in a neutral position. Repeat this exercise as you draw attention to your breath, muscles, and movement for five repetitions.

Disciplined Attitude

Thomas Edison is credited with saying, "Opportunity is missed by most because it is dressed in overalls and looks like work." That work—aka discipline—is the greatest barrier to following through on mindful attentiveness. If your body signals danger, fatigue, unhealthy weight gain, soreness, etc., and you don't follow through with action, what good will the attentiveness be?

My students often ask me how to deal with any number of these signals, usually after they have seen a doctor or gone on diets. Many of them want to pursue radical changes, and their eyes are resolute. When I tell them what they need to do in order to care for their bodies—whether it be to lose weight, correct their balance or posture, or alleviate lower back pain, they listen with wide eyes. Some students come with a good attitude, brimming with determination. The success rate that I have witnessed

Seated Warm-up

in these students has been remarkably high. I know that their results are directly linked to their mindful attentiveness of the signals their body sent, their positive attitudes, and their commitment to change.

I remember one young lady, Sara, who started attending my classes three times a week in an effort to lose one hundred pounds. Honestly, I didn't know if she was capable of sticking with the relatively intensive exercise program. But I was pleasantly surprised when she consistently attended the aerobics classes and even started going to my evening Pilates classes and taking up cycling. Within a year, Sara had lost the one hundred pounds. During that year, what I noticed most about her was that her attitude was outstanding. She always wore a warm, sincere smile, and she seemed at peace with herself.

A few months after Sara lost the excess weight, I encouraged her to become certified in Pilates, which she did. I was overwhelmed with joy for her—she had heard her body's call to change and taken action.

Some of my students, however, look at me like I'm insane when I offer advice about responding to their bodies' warning signs. They can't imagine putting in the amount of effort I recommend, and they leave discouraged and paralyzed.

One of the biggest lies our culture tells us is that good health is easily attainable. Pills

> "One of the biggest lies our culture tells us is that good health is easily attainable. Pills are suggested for weight loss, and different pills are recommended for pain. But our bodies are often a better resource than we think, more able to permanently care for our health issues than medication."

are suggested for weight loss, and different pills are recommended for pain. But our bodies are often a better resource than we think, more able to permanently care for our health issues than medication. Careful stretching and weight lifting will correct back pain a million times faster than any pain killer. And, just as Sara demonstrated, consistent exercise will take unwanted weight off better than any diet pill on the market.

Pursuing weight loss or caring for challenging health problems may feel hopeless to many people, but with the right attitude, you can achieve anything you set your mind to. That is the promise of mindful attentiveness: If you diagnose your problem by listening to your body's signals, and if you follow through with determined action, you will accomplish your goal. What you believe to be true will motivate you, regardless of how challenging that road may appear.

Theresa's Top Three for Listening

1 Choose a phrase that describes an attitude you want to have and listen to yourself repeat it several times each day. Like a barbell for your mind, it will help you become stronger in maintaining a positive, healthy attitude.

2 Pay attention to your body's cues. From lethargy and soreness to pain, don't take your body's language lightly. Listen and respond.

3 Listen to God. Get in tune with Him through reading His Word and through prayer and communication.

Shaped by God

Our body's signals are unique—different from any diagnoses a doctor can give. Doctors are necessary—they are healers—but they can't feel what we feel. They can't hear what our bodies are saying as clearly as we can. The same is true for spiritual attentiveness. In order to hear from God, we have to be able to distinguish His voice from others. And the only way to recognize the voice of God is to know Him intimately through His written Word and through daily communication.

When I started to study God's Word daily, I began to hear Him speak to me through different Scriptures and in my prayer time. In time, I also began depending on Him for everything, instead of only asking a friend's help or opinion. I always pray for direction and wisdom, and God acknowledges these requests in His perfect timing. When we seek God, He will speak to us. I am dependent on hearing from Him on a daily basis, just like I am dependent on listening to my physical body in exercise.

"It takes commitment to hear God speak."

And just as exercise requires commitment, it also takes commitment to hear God speak. Perhaps before you warm up your body for a workout, you can do a ten-minute warm-up for your spirit as well by reading in Psalms or Proverbs. Begin in prayer, and then pay close attention to what He might be saying to you through His Word. He is always available to you, but it is up to you to discipline your spirit through prayer, listening, studying, and obeying. And as you begin to see results in your body, God will reward your spiritual efforts as well when you seek

His voice. You'll start to see and hear the signs of God all around you, in peace, patience, humility, commitment and joy, and others will notice the changes in both your body and spirit. Matthew 13:16 says, "Blessed are your eyes, because they see; and your ears, because they hear" (NIV).

Shaped by Prayer

LORD JESUS, I LOVE YOU SO MUCH. MY SOUL
YEARNS TO HEAR YOUR VOICE DAILY. HELP
ME TO OPEN UP THE EYES AND EARS OF MY
HEART AS I LISTEN IN THE STILLNESS OF THE
DAY. TEACH ME TO BE SENSITIVE TO HEARING
YOU WHEN YOU SPEAK. ALLOW ME THE
ABILITY TO BE ABLE TO DISTINGUISH YOUR
VOICE AMONG THE CHATTER. I PRAY THAT YOU
WOULD GRANT ME THE WISDOM
AND DISCERNMENT TO UNDERSTAND WHAT
YOU ARE COMMUNICATING TO ME. MAY MY
MIND, HEART, AND BODY BE IN TUNE WITH
YOUR HOLY SPIRIT. TO YOU BE THE GLORY
FOREVER AND EVER, AMEN.

Chapter Two

Breathe

"THE SPIRIT OF GOD HAS MADE ME; THE BREATH
OF THE ALMIGHTY GIVES ME LIFE."

JOB 33:4 (NIV)

The act of breathing is simple: Inhale oxygen and exhale carbon dioxide. But for such a simple act, it's one of the most necessary functions of our bodies. We can go days or weeks without water or food, but without oxygen, we would die in mere minutes.

From the moment I was born, I knew how to breathe. But many times in my life, I experienced moments when breathing didn't come so easily, so I began to discover the *practice* of breathing. I breathe to live, I breathe to maximize exercise, and I breathe to take in the breath of the Almighty. Learning to breathe as a practice is available for everyone who's willing to pay attention to the way they inhale and exhale. Once you decide to practice breathing, your body has the opportunity to be transformed into a living spiritual vessel that sustains you.

Shaped by Life

During the spring of my freshman year in high school, my mother was suddenly sent to the local hospital. My dad told me that she was fine; the doctors just wanted to run some tests. But after my mother spent a week in the hospital, I knew things were not fine at all.

In what I thought was an attempt to ease our minds, my father informed my younger brother Paul and me that we were taking a summer trip to Houston, Texas. We all loaded up the Oldsmobile and headed south from Kentucky. I remember that we made a lot of stops to look at the sights and to give my mother some fresh air. She looked really weak on the trip but didn't complain.

Once we made it to Houston, we checked into a high-rise hotel with a swimming pool on the roof. But my mother would not be staying with us in the hotel for very long. Shortly after our so-called vacation began, we were visiting the MD Anderson Cancer Center. My mother had cancer.

During the time we were in Houston, my father rarely took Paul and me to visit our mother in the hospital. I think she had undergone a few surgeries, and my father did not want us to worry about her. But one particular visit to the hospital stands out in my memory—when my father's admonition not to worry was impossible to obey. Walking through the doors of this larger-than-life hospital, I saw a lot of sick and pitifully thin people. I had never been exposed to anyone with cancer before, and my stomach tightened as we made our way to the elevator. I told myself that my mother would be fine and our life would be back to normal soon.

But when I first saw her painfully thin body and bald head, I lost my breath. Literally, for a moment, I couldn't breathe. After what felt like a long period of breathlessness, I tried to recover, acting as if it didn't really bother me to see her this way. I told her how Paul and I had met a lot of nice kids at the hotel and swam with them each day. Looking back now, I can see the compassion in my mother's eyes; she knew I was in shock.

She told me that she wanted my help picking out a wig, and I said that I would be glad to do that. I think she asked me to help her because she could see I wanted to do something, and there was little I could do. For the first time, I realized the fragility of life. Looking at her gaunt body and bare head, my heart fell—but somehow, I was inspired at the same time. The confidence in her voice assured me that she wouldn't give up, even though she was going through a lot of agony and pain.

My mother was released from the hospital, and we returned home just in time for me to begin my sophomore year. I had dance practice after school, but when I returned home, the first thing I did was visit my mother. I would slowly climb the stairs to her room, my heart rate increasing and my breathing growing heavy. I almost always found her resting in bed, so I would sit beside her, and we would chat. I didn't know then just how much I would forever cherish those moments with her.

Instead of getting better, my mother's health continued to deteriorate. My father bought a hospital bed and placed it in their bedroom, right in front of the window, so that she could feel the warmth of the sun. Mom had always loved the outdoors, and she particularly enjoyed playing golf with my father on the weekends. The cute golfing skirts and matching tops always looked so fashionable and crisp on her, and I remember desperately wanting to see her in those clothes again.

By October, things began to rapidly change. After school, I would rush home, jumping two steps at a time to get to my mother's side for our daily chats. Mom would try to open her eyes, but she would fall in and out of sleep as I spoke. Her breathing was shallow; her chest rose and fell rapidly. Occasionally, she would stop breathing for what seemed like minutes, and then, finally, exhale.

"Mom, I want you to live," I said to her on one particularly challenging night. "I have so much to tell you each day. Please don't die on me."

But in November, the air turned crisp and frigid, and my mother did not know who I was.

The night she died was surreal. As I climbed the stairs, I felt as if I were walking a gauntlet. I didn't want to enter the bedroom and see her dead. Everything inside of me was rumbling. I caught a glimpse of my father in the hallway, and he was wiping tears from his face, holding his glasses in his other hand.

"Go kiss her good-bye," my father said.

I didn't want to. Kissing a dead person seemed so morbid and scary to me. My father came over and nudged me forward to the bed where my mother lay. He again told me to kiss her good-bye. I respectfully obeyed his wishes.

I'm glad I wasn't home to witness my mother's last breath, because I can only see her alive in my memory. I like to remember my mom in her golfing outfit, walking with my dad on the golf course for another round.

Theresa's Top Three for Breathing

1 Prayerfully revisit a time when you bottled up your emotions. Take special care to breathe deeply all the while, releasing the tension of that memory, making your body feel safe, and inviting healing into your heart.

2 Find a quiet place and pray. Breathe your prayers to God. Exhale your confessions, and inhale His love and forgiveness.

3 Release tension in your body by bringing awareness to your breath all day long. When you feel tension, take a moment to focus on breathing deeply.

Shaped by Fitness

Reflecting back on my life, I realize now that I began a dangerous practice of restricting my breath when I watched my mother's health deteriorate. As a child, I released my stress and tension through crying or laughing out loud. But at fourteen, with my mother dying, I felt like I needed to grow up quickly and constrain my emotions. I know now that when I lost my breath in my mother's hospital room, I simply didn't want her to see me looking sad or unsupportive. Similarly, in later moments of fear or shock, I often lost my breath again. At times I have felt like my heart and lungs were ready to explode.

It wasn't until I looked back that I realized how much bottling up my emotions—and thus my breaths—could hurt me. As I began my life in fitness, I found out that in order to survive my first aerobics classes—and the difficulties in life that were to come—I had to pay close attention to my breathing. Since then, I've learned the importance of effective breathing. We can no more get through an exercise program without breath than we can a difficult, exciting, or terrifying experience. Stressful situations cause us to tense up and shallowly breathe. But applying deep, focused, rhythmic and cleansing breathing to our daily lives is a powerful way to release our emotions and tension, exercise more effectively, and pray. All of us experience breathless moments, but we can more joyfully endure trials when we learn to harness our breath and flow into the next seasons of our lives.

> "Shallow breathing prevents your body from getting enough oxygen, which leaves you at risk for heart attacks, cancer, strokes and other diseases."

Deep Breathing Exercise

Learning how to breathe properly, particularly while exercising, will help you focus on your muscles and your body while burning fat at the same time. As we inhale, the oxygen goes to our lungs and then into our bloodstreams. Exhaling, carbon dioxide leaves our body and is put back into the air. Chest breathing (shallow breaths) hinders our body's ability to release enough carbon dioxide, and all that stored carbon dioxide in our bodies causes a real problem with cell metabolization, brain function and weight gain. Shallow breathing also prevents your body from getting enough oxygen, which leaves you at risk for heart attacks, cancer, strokes and other diseases and will eventually lead to muscle atrophy and exercise intolerance.

But if we pay close attention to our breathing, both in exercise and in everyday life, we can garner huge benefits for our bodies. One of the best ways to begin that awareness is to practice deep breathing.

Deep breathing is one of the most beneficial exercises we can do for our bodies. Yes, deep breathing is exercise! As we breathe deeply from our diaphragm, the muscles of our abdominals and intestines are massaged and strengthened. Bringing awareness to our breath nourishes every cell in our body. One of the many wonderful facts—and best-kept secrets—about deep breathing is that it naturally increases our metabolism. When we increase the oxygen in our cells, our metabolism kicks into high gear and we become more energized. And, of course, jump-starting our metabolism will help us lose weight if necessary or maintain a healthy body weight.

Deep breathing also promotes circulation and helps our lymphatic system work more efficiently. Every cell in our body is surrounded by a fluid called lymph, and our lymphatic system works as a sewage system by removing dead cells, blood proteins and other toxic materials. Conscious breathing detoxifies our bodies and renews our minds and spirits.

Practicing deep breathing will raise our levels of blood oxygen and stimulate our metabolism while improving our fitness and mental performance. Our brains need three times more oxygen than the rest of our organs. Without enough oxygen, the brain becomes oxygen deprived, the body becomes weak, and the brain starts to shut down. Deep breathing also helps to turn our deposits of fat into body fuel while increasing our energy level. If you are constantly tired, have low energy, and deal with bouts of depression, your brain and body might be oxygen starved. You can do something about this today: Learn how to take care of your body's health through deep breathing.

Many of us are so busy that we never even think about breathing. The good news is that deep breathing is one form of exercise you can do anywhere, anytime. You can practice deep breathing while you are driving in your car, waiting at the doctor's office, sitting at your desk, doing laundry, grocery shopping, at church, taking a shower, listening to friends . . . any time! I love to practice deep breathing while driving. It helps me ease any muscle tension I may be experiencing in my neck or shoulders. If you spend a lot of time driving from one place to another, this may be a great place to start practicing your breathing.

There are several effective deep breathing exercises. The simplest version is to take a deep inhale through your nose while raising your shoulders toward your ears. Next, slowly exhale out of your mouth as you gently press your shoulders down. Repeat this deep breathing exercise five more times and notice the tension leaving your body. The more you practice this exercise, the less muscle tension you will experience. It's a little-known fact that the power of relieving this neck and shoulder tension lies in your breath.

Here is a more involved deep breathing exercise you can do just about anywhere:

Sit comfortably in a chair or choose to lie down and close your eyes. To begin, inhale fully through your mouth and then release all the air. Next, deeply inhale through your nose as you direct the oxygen to fill the lungs, sides, and back. You should notice your belly expanding during the inhale as you count to five. Then, slowly exhale out of your mouth and notice the breath deep within the belly making its way up toward the chest and out of your mouth as your belly tightens. Try to exhale longer as you wring out every ounce of air from your lungs. After you become familiar with this exercise, you may choose to close your eyes and relax through each breath. Remember you can do this exercise anywhere, anyplace. Repeat this deep breathing sequence five to ten times or as many times as you would like. If you have trouble sleeping, try this exercise before bed to help assist with sound sleep. Over time, you will find that your body craves more oxygen, and deep breathing will come naturally.

Focused Breathing

Allowing our breath to help us during a challenging workout makes it easier on our bodies as well. When my students jump rope or do jumping jacks, for example, I remind them to "go hard easy." As we focus on our breath, it makes it easier for our physical body to work harder. Our muscles do not tense up when we rely on our breath to move us. Keeping our minds focused on our breathing while jumping rope or doing challenging workouts releases the tension in the muscles, and, in turn,

> • • •
>
> "Keeping our minds focused on our breathing while jumping rope or doing challenging workouts releases the tension in the muscles, and, in turn, the muscles and body are able to work harder and longer."
>
> • • •

the muscles and body are able to work harder and longer. This occurs because with focused rhythmic breathing, we are properly supplying oxygen to the muscles and the rest of the body.

As we pay attention to our breath while exercising, our mind and muscles team up to work more efficiently. Some people hold or force their breathing as a way of handling intensity, but holding your breath while exercising is dangerous. It can increase your blood pressure rapidly and cause painful exercise-induced headaches. Holding your breath may even cause you to faint.

If you are lifting weights at home or in the gym, there is a proper breathing pattern that needs to occur. Before you begin lifting weights, make sure you have good posture and body alignment. If you are standing, sitting, or lying down, always focus on keeping your spine (back) neutral (elongated). Also, make sure that you are contracting your abdominals (holding them in) without holding your breath. Good posture is a prerequisite for strength training and deep breathing.

So what does focused, rhythmic breathing look like? Suppose you are going to do a basic shoulder press. After you have checked your posture, inhale deeply through your nose and position the weights on each side of your shoulders with your elbows below your wrists. Next, exhale and press both weights over your head until your arms are fully extended.

Then inhale and lower the weights back down to your shoulders. Notice that the exhale occurs while you are lifting the weights overhead because this is the hardest part of the exercise. The deep inhale happens during the easiest part of the exercise. Let your breath dictate the speed and pace at which you perform exercises. A good rule of thumb is to always exhale on the hardest part of the exercise and inhale while doing the easier part of the exercise. This rule will help you in whatever style of workout you choose to do.

Let's switch gears and talk about breathing during cardiovascular exercise. Natural rhythmic breathing will help you jump, skip, run, swim, bicycle, walk, or anything else you choose to do. Because there is a high demand placed on our bodies for more oxygen during cardiovascular exercise, it is best to keep your mouth open and your face relaxed. When you relax the face and jaw, the rest of the muscles and the body will move freely without strain. Tensing the muscles in your face while working out will cause too much energy expenditure in the upper body and possibly cause you to hold your breath. Relaxing your face allows your breath to move in and out of your lungs with ease.

Power walking is a particularly good way to work on rhythmic breathing. Start off by standing tall, exhale first, and then start walking with your lead foot. Take four steps while inhaling deeply, and then take four steps while exhaling. Use each step as a count or inhale. The breathing should be done in a continuous flow. You can do this rhythmic breathing exercise while walking at a park or in the grocery store, descending a flight of stairs, running outside or on the treadmill, on your way to lunch, or whenever you think of it. Developing the habit of rhythmic breathing during cardiovascular exercise will help slow your heart rate and allow you to prolong your exercise. If, however, you notice that your breathing feels out of control, be sure to slow down, and take a few deep breaths independent of the exercise. When you feel like your breathing is back to a more manageable pace, resume the exercise.

When I began running, I had to retrain my body to breathe. I found that if I used rhythmic breathing, my breaths took on a natural cadence. The cadence helped me stay focused and keep a good pace.

I eventually added a prayerful element to my rhythmic breathing, saying a word over and over with each breath. Most often, the word that I would repeat would be direct and to the point: "Jesus . . . Jesus . . . Jesus." Sometimes, I would use a phrase like, "Jesus . . . You are . . . the Lord . . . of my . . . life." Often, by the time my run was over, I had been so focused on my praise chant that I had nearly forgotten about the workout. Finding your natural breathing pattern while doing cardio will absolutely prove a rewarding practice for you. Full, deep breathing has a profound impact on all aspects of our health. Not only will rhythmic breathing help you to stay focused while exercising, it also helps the body and muscles to perform naturally without tension or stress.

Now, let's consider the physical benefits of cleansing breaths. Deep breathing helps us decrease anxiety, depression, pain, and fatigue. Most adults, as they age,

● ● ●

"Cleansing breaths help us to stay fit by regulating our heart rate and blood pressure and by improving our circulation, digestive system and nervous system."

● ● ●

breathe more shallowly and rapidly than they did as children, who naturally breathe deeply and move easily. Cleansing breaths help us to stay fit by regulating our heart rate and blood pressure and by improving our circulation, digestive system and nervous system. If we practice deep breathing every day, it will become a habit and a way of breathing for life.

Focused breathing can also help us kick some unhealthy habits. Several of my students have told me that they have been able to stop smoking by making a habit of exercising. I love to share with them the fact that combining deep rhythmic breathing with exercising is the reason behind their decreased need to smoke. Once a person learns how to breathe deeply, the urge to smoke fades significantly.

Flow Exercise Breathing

Discovering flow exercise breathing—primarily through Pilates—has helped me to better handle stress and tension.

By placing emphasis on our breathing, we are diverted from focusing on stressful events because breathing helps the mind slow down and relax. I have learned to harness my breath by focusing on the way I am breathing. This breathing technique gives me strength and helps relieve tension in my body. I also love Pilates breathing because it calms me down before bed and helps me relax from head to toe.

Pilates asks you to inhale through your nose as you prepare to move into an exercise and to exhale out of your mouth as you gracefully move through the exercise. This purposeful breathing, called diaphragmatic breathing, helps enhance the execution of our movements.

Here's one flow exercise—the Pilates Hundred—that will help you focus on breathing and challenge your abdominals at the same time. This exercise is used as a dynamic warm-up for the abdominals and lungs.

1. Lie on your back (supine) with your knees bent and your feet flat on the floor, your arms by your sides. Inhale through your nose five counts and gently press your lower back to the floor.

2. Exhale out of your mouth as you contract your abdominals, lift your head and shoulders up, and gaze at your belly.

3. Hold your position and inhale through your nose for five counts. Exhale, pulling your naval closer to your spine and lifting your arms off the floor a few inches, with fingertips extended.

4. Inhale as you prepare to advance the leg position and exhale as you place both of your legs in a ninety-degree angle (tabletop position). Gazing toward your belly, pump your arms up and down by your sides in a controlled manner. Inhale five short breaths through your nose and exhale five short breaths out of your mouth. The arms pump in unison with your breath. Keep your shoulders and neck relaxed and abdominals engaged.

5. Do a cycle of ten full breaths. Each cycle is five short inhales and five short exhales.

6. If you are an advanced Pilates enthusiast, try pumping while extending your legs (keeping your heels together) straight up toward the ceiling and then lowering your legs toward the floor, maintaining a neutral spine. Do not lower your legs past the point where your spine starts to lift off the floor.

If you are a first timer, start the Pilates Hundred by simply keeping your feet flat on the floor.

Shaped by God

I used to experience a lot of gut-wrenching stomachaches as a child. The doctors couldn't find anything wrong and told my mother that I was just fine. I now believe that fear—religious fear—was the trigger for my stomachaches. We were strict Catholics, and I would worry about going to hell if I didn't attend mass on Sunday, and I couldn't keep all of those sins in different degrees and levels straight. Mortal and venial sins and medium-sized sins made my head spin and my stomach hurt. The priest told us if we confessed our sins to him and prayed a few specific prayers like the "Hail Mary," our sins would be forgiven until we sinned again. I couldn't handle that type of pressure; I knew I was going to sin again and again.

• • •

"I can breathe easy knowing that I can go straight to Jesus, confess my sins, be cleansed of them, and be set free."

• • •

As I studied the Word and grew older, I realized that God was available to hear my confessions and prayers whether I was talking to a priest or in my car. Today, I can breathe easy knowing that I can go straight to Jesus, confess my sins, be cleansed of them, and be set free.

In just about everything I do, I combine spiritual and physical practices to develop my wholeness. Cleansing breaths is one of those practices. Confessing our sins is the first step to cleansing our souls from the toxic waste that attaches itself to our bodies. It also helps us deal with painful situations—like the mourning I went through for my mother. Deeply exhaling our sins to God can bring healing. The Word of God tells us that He forgives us our sins if we confess them to Him. To practice confession prayers, combine the deep breathing exercises from this chapter with a prayerful, repentant heart. Allow your mind to ask for forgiveness as you exhale the sins from your soul.

Here is an example of how to combine your breath with confession. You may want to reflect on the following prayer before you get started.

· · ·

HAVE MERCY ON ME, O GOD, BECAUSE OF YOUR UNFAILING LOVE. BECAUSE OF YOUR GREAT COMPASSION, BLOT OUT THE STAIN OF MY SINS. WASH ME CLEAN FROM MY GUILT. PURIFY ME FROM MY SIN.
PSALM 51:1-2

· · ·

Begin by sitting or lying down in a quiet place as you bring awareness to your breath. You may enjoy listening to soothing music during this exercise. Pay close attention to how your breath is moving in and out of your body. Recognize that God is in the air that you breathe as you prepare your lungs. Close your eyes and take a deep inhale through your nose, and imagine God filling your lungs with His breath. Exhale and reflect on any unconfessed sin in your life. Take another deep inhale and notice tension or stress in the forehead, neck or shoulder area. Slowly exhale out this tension as you continue to confess your sins to

God. Notice the cleansing that is taking place within your body and soul as you breathe and pray. Repeat this exercise for another ten cleansing breaths.

After breathing confession prayers, do the same with a different mind-set: a forgiving mind-set. Exhale the waste of grudges and bitterness from your body and focus on forgiving others who have hurt you. The disciples asked Jesus, "How many times do we forgive, seven times?" Christ answered, "Seven times seventy." I believe seven times seventy means to live a life of forgiveness, and Jesus will be your cleansing breath.

Jesus made it possible for us to walk in peace and love others by showing how much He loved us. Peace can be ours if our hearts are not closed and hard. But we need to forgive ourselves first, and this will open the door to our hearts. Proverbs says, "A heart at peace gives life to the body" (NIV). If we are at peace with ourselves, we can then begin to open the door of peace to others.

Prayer as Breathing

When life has been emotionally and physically challenging, I could always depend on my breath to keep me alive. Naturally, we all need oxygen for life, but I am talking about real life through spiritual breathing. In other words, prayer. Prayer releases God's power and strength into our lives and changes us from the inside out.

Prayer has become my spiritual breath—just as inhaling and exhaling support our bodies, so does prayer support our spirit. Praying keeps me alive and refreshes my soul through direct communication with God. God's Word instructs us in 1 Thessalonians 5:17–18 to "pray continually; give thanks in all circumstances, for this is God's will for you in Christ Jesus" (NIV).

I have learned that God moves in and out of us with each breath we take. It is up to each of us to inhale what is good in this life and to exhale what is not so good. Turning our hearts, minds, and spirits toward God opens up the lines of communication between us and our Creator. When we draw close to Him, He draws close to us.

> "Prayer has become my spiritual breath—just as inhaling and exhaling support our bodies, so does prayer support our spirit."

Anyone can pray at any time, day or night. In order to pray, we need to start with a clean heart by asking God to forgive us of any un-confessed sin. If you want to experience prayer with your heavenly Father, invite Him to communicate with you when you communicate with Him, and begin by thanking Him for who He is. As we begin to harmonize with God through prayer, He opens the door of peace and comfort to our souls.

I survived some of the most difficult times in my life by communicating with God through constant prayer. God is here for all of us—all we have to do is ask Him to enter our hearts and breathe His peace and goodness into our lives. In Matthew, Jesus tells us, "Ask and it will be given to you; seek and you will find; knock and the door will be opened to you. For everyone who asks receives; he who seeks finds; and to him who knocks, the door will be opened" (NIV). Don't give up in seeking God through prayer; continue to seek and pray, and you will be rewarded for your efforts. As we mature in our prayer life, we begin to pray for things that are honoring to God.

Shaped by Prayer

JESUS, YOU ARE MY SOURCE OF OXYGEN.
YOU ARE THE ONLY TRUE BREATH OF LIFE
THAT I BREATHE EACH DAY. FORGIVE ME
OF MY SINS, LORD, AND CLEANSE ME FROM
HEAD TO TOE. HELP ME TO FORGIVE
THOSE WHO HAVE HURT ME, AND TEACH
ME HOW TO LOVE MY ENEMIES. I STRIVE TO BE
MORE LIKE YOU EACH DAY. GRANT ME
THE STRENGTH TO CONTINUE MOVING
FORWARD WHEN LIFE BECOMES DIFFICULT.
HELP ME TO NOT HOLD MY BREATH, BUT
FILL MY LUNGS WITH YOUR GOODNESS
AND MERCY. ALLOW ME THE WISDOM AND
THE STRENGTH TO HELP OTHERS WHO ARE
HURTING. I PRAY THAT YOU WOULD USE MY
LIFE AS I'M DANCING,
MOVING AND BREATHING,
TO BRING GLORY TO YOUR NAME.
IN THE NAME OF JESUS CHRIST I PRAY,
AMEN.

Chapter Three

Partner

HIS UNCHANGING PLAN HAS ALWAYS BEEN TO
ADOPT US INTO HIS OWN FAMILY BY BRINGING US
TO HIMSELF THROUGH JESUS CHRIST. . . .

EPHESIANS 1:5

Partnerships can be found in the most unexpected places. In fact, no matter where we go—even without noticing it—we are affected by partnerships big and small. When we buy a gallon of milk, we partner with the farmer who produced it. When we drive to work, we partner with the state, using the roads it provides and, in turn, following the rules it sets. And when we pray with a friend, Scripture promises that, somehow, God is glorified. God Himself makes up the most powerful partnership of all: the holy Trinity.

Similarly, partnerships have an unexpected but profound effect on our workouts. Workout partners motivate us exponentially more than we could ourselves. Plus, they share in our misery—something we humans tend to appreciate—and our joy in accomplishment.

Depending on how we treat them, our collaborations can prove to be positive or negative . . . but they will always be powerful. I've experienced the effects of partnerships good and bad throughout my life. The stories that I want to share with you now are the partnerships that led to my being adopted, and, later, the ones that nearly forced me to give up my first child.

Shaped by Life

In many cases, adoption is one of the happiest words there is—it means that infertility or unwanted pregnancy is transformed into a beautiful blessing. But nonetheless, adoption is still bred from tragedy, whether it's a teenage or single mother who has to give up her child, or a child who's been orphaned or born into poverty. And the possibilities of tragedy stretch down the line to adopted children who, like me, feel abandoned. Being both "abandoned" by my birth mother and adopted by my parents, my heart has almost always been in a constant battle of tug-of-war. The love I had for my adoptive family could not quite counterbalance the homesickness I felt for my mother's touch.

I met my birth mother when I was in my thirties and found out that she had been forced by her family and her boyfriend's family to put me up for adoption because she was not married, and her family was worried about the many repercussions of her having a child out of wedlock. The families' partnership became a great negative force, leaving her with empty arms that ached for her child and leaving me with feelings of abandonment. Even now, forty-five years later, her voice carries a sadness recalling those memories. She told me that she spent months waiting for her true love to rescue her, to save her from having to give me up. He never came. She describes giving birth to me as my being taken and rushed away. She never got to see her reflection in my baby-blue eyes, and six weeks later, I was adopted by a Catholic family from Hopkinsville, Kentucky.

I loved my adopted family, but my parents were very strict, and I spent a lot of my childhood in fear.

One of my earliest recollections of life with my family involved my older brother Danny and his incredible ability to exasperate my mother. My mother was preparing dinner while I sat at the window, waiting for my father to return home from work. When Dad arrived home, we all sat down for dinner. Dad sat at one end of the table and Mom at the other. Everything appeared perfectly normal to me, but evidently Danny did something to provoke my mother. In one swift motion, she picked up the Heinz 57 bottle and launched it with precise accuracy at my brother, striking him right between the eyes. The force of the blow knocked him backward and onto the floor.

In those days, grocers used a blue ink stamp to price their products, and right in the middle of Danny's forehead was the most recent price of the sauce. I spoke about this story with Danny recently, and he recalled the event with laughter. He said, "I guess I really ticked her off that time." As a four-year-old, I was probably more affected by the incident than Danny. It was just another reason for me to be afraid.

Not only were my parents strict with the way the home was run—for example, in the summer, we would have "two-a-days," only breakfast and dinner—they were also quite conservative—so conservative that they believed mass should be done in Latin and that anything less than Latin was a sin. And, of course, each of us children attended a very strict and conservative Catholic school. Practically every element of my training as a child taught me to fear my parents and to fear church.

After my mother's death, my father shut down in every way, and I acquired the role of surrogate mother to my brother Paul and housekeeper to my father. I would grocery shop, cook, clean the house and try to make my father happy again. Cleaning seemed to help purge my pain, though my pain stemmed less from my mother's death and more from watching my father quietly give up. I had always looked to my father for inner strength, but that had disappeared.

Theresa's Top Three for Partnering

1 Work out with an exercise partner or a group fitness class a few days a week. You will be more willing to exercise when you know someone is counting on you to show up.

2 Choose a prayer partner, someone who will pray for and with you, who will challenge you to grow in knowledge.

3 Know that God is your partner in every activity and every endeavor. He will give you strength.

With my dad preoccupied by his own pain, I went to college without much guidance and plunged headfirst into a new relationship. My father offered no wise counsel about young men and how I should conduct myself in relationships with them. I made decisions based on my feelings and became engrossed in my newfound love.

I spent most of my time with my boyfriend, Brian, in his dorm room. I knew that our careless physical relationship might get us in trouble, so I decided to see the school nurse about birth control. The nurse called later that day and said that it was too late for birth control. . . . I was pregnant.

When I explained the situation to Brian, he couldn't believe it either. How were we going to tell our parents? Both of us just sat there, wondering what to do next. I felt like I had just ruined my life. Although we cared deeply for one another, we both agreed we were too young for marriage.

When I returned home, I sensed that, somehow, my father already knew about the pregnancy. He approached me with the question, and I admitted the truth. Much to my surprise, he commended me for not using birth control. I found that shocking—he had never been an encouraging person or complimented me on any of my achievements, and, yet, he was congratulating me on not using birth control.

He asked if we had considered marriage, and I told him we both felt we were too young. He reminded me that we certainly had not been too young to have intimate relations, so maybe we were not too young to get married. I just wanted to raise my child and go on with life. But Dad was quite forceful: If there were no marriage, the child must be given up for adoption. He would not allow me to live in his house and raise the child on my own. I was so naïve, and I thought there were no choices other than the ones he offered me. Little did I know then how closely my story resembled my birth mother's.

I could tell that my father and his new wife were embarrassed by my pregnancy, and so were Brian's parents. My father resigned from some of his social involvements, and Brian's parents would not allow him to see me. Looking at the situation today, the families formed a partnership mirroring the partnership that forced my mother to give me away. Undeterred, Brian would sneak over in the evenings to discuss a plan to keep our baby. We decided that he would join the Air Force so that he could support our baby until we were ready to get married. We hoped to form a positive partnership to overwhelm the negative influences of the families.

But my father insisted that we visit Catholic Charities in Louisville, Kentucky, the same place where my biological mother had stayed and had given me up for adoption. The nuns and lay people seemed nice enough, but my heart and stomach groaned, knowing this was the place where I had been given away. I didn't want my child to go through all those years of feeling abandoned like I had. I understand now how partnering with adoption services provides a positive collaboration for many families and children, but I was there against my will—I wanted to keep my baby.

Finally, the thirteenth of June came, my due date. After twenty-four hours of labor, my daughter was born. Christina was absolutely perfect. When her little blue eyes looked into mine, I knew I could never give her up.

The next day, a lady from Catholic Charities showed up in my room. She explained that my daughter would be well taken care of and that she was already promised to a lovely family. My father told me it was time to sign the papers and give the baby to the agency, and he became very angry when I refused. At that point, I really didn't care what he thought of me. But because I had already made arrangements—and somehow the law required it—the lady from Catholic Charities took my child away. They even refused to pass the message of my daughter's birth along to Brian, who was at Air Force boot camp, because we were not married.

I couldn't look at my father; there were no words to describe how numb I felt at that moment. My dad brought me home, and I stayed in my bedroom, staring at the walls. He tried to get me to eat, but I refused.

A couple of days later, he and his wife left together for a social get-together. While he was gone, the phone rang, and I jumped to answer it. It was Brian. My heart raced as I explained everything that had happened with the baby. He asked me if I wanted to get married and, of course, I said yes. I wanted to rescue my daughter, and time was running out. Within a few weeks he would be finished with boot camp, and he could then fly home to get married. Honestly, we had made some bad decisions that put us in this situation, but we were attempting to work together to save our daughter.

When my father and his wife came home, I anxiously told them the great news. My father told me he didn't believe me. In fact, he said he would not believe the story until he heard it from Brian, over the phone. I explained to my father that Brian would not be allowed to call again during boot camp, but he didn't believe that either.

I didn't know Christ as my savior in those days, but with all my soul, I cried out to Him. I asked Him for a miracle: that Brian be allowed just one more phone call.

The next morning, our phone rang, and I heard my father speaking with Brian. My dad calmly got off the phone, and he told me to get ready to drive to Louisville. We were bringing Christina home.

Shaped by Fitness

That story, along with other stories in my life, has taught me just how powerful partnerships can be. My adoptive parents worked together to provide a home for me and turn a devastating situation into a productive collaboration. And when Brian and I joined together to save our daughter, we created a fusion that kept her in my arms and saved my heart from being irrevocably crushed. Even though we were immature—and neither one of us had characters of steel—we accomplished something together that we could never have done as individuals.

So it is with partners in fitness. Choosing workout partners or groups heightens your motivation, strength and stamina so much more than when you exercise alone.

One of the advantages of teaching fitness classes is that I get to work out with a variety of people every day. My workouts are never boring, because my students bring their unique personalities to the class. I consider my students to be my workout partners, because we share the common bond of keeping our bodies physically fit. Regardless of your current workout routine (or lack thereof), a partner can help keep your workout fresh and challenging. Here are some things you can begin looking for in a fitness partner.

Your partner should have similar fitness goals and be committed to

> **"** Choosing workout partners or groups heightens your motivation, strength and stamina so much more than when you exercise alone. **"**

showing up and working hard. Ideally, you will find someone who won't quit in the middle of a workout, and who will encourage you to go further than you thought possible. This type of partner will feed off your accomplishments and will be motivating to you with a positive "can do" attitude. Both of you will look forward to the next workout and want the best for each other. It will not take long to discover if you have the right workout partner. If someone frequently stands you up, complains about the length of the workout, suggests coffee and doughnuts while working out . . . then it's time to find another partner.

It is also important to find someone at your fitness level or higher. A fit partner is dependable and will push harder to help you to reach your fitness goals faster.

Understanding is a good quality to look for in a fitness partner. An understanding person knows when to back off and when to push hard.

Even dogs can be great workout partners! They need exercise, too, and taking them with you for a walk or a run is a great way to keep both of you in good shape. Besides, they are very loyal and unlikely to sleep in when you want to work out.

I have also found that working out with the same gender is more productive. Opposite gender fitness partners don't often mix well. Besides the fact that you'll likely be at different fitness levels, there's of course the added tension of the sexes, which can be distracting. (Of course, if you've chosen a man as your workout partner *because* you hope to ignite some flames, that's fine . . . but don't expect maximized workouts!)

Choosing a partner is one of the best ways to stay motivated and keep moving forward. Together, you both can succeed. In Ecclesiastes 4, we're encouraged to team up with a partner so that we can help each other: "Two people are better off than one, for they can help each other succeed. If one person falls, the other can reach out and help."

Partner Circuit Workout

Since you now know what to look for in an exercise partner, I thought it might be helpful to give you an exercise plan that you can do together. This particular workout can be done inside or outside. I like to take this workout to the park and enjoy the beauty of nature.

It is important to stay hydrated during the workout. And please feel free to modify the exercises to fit your fitness level and goals.

See Chapter 4, "Stretch," for information on the elastic band.
See Chapter 8, "Balance," for information on the stability ball.

stability ball chest press
with elastic band

If you don't have a stability ball, use a raised platform or bench instead.
Lie down on a stability ball in a bridge position—middle back on the ball,
legs bent at a ninety-degree angle with feet flat on the floor. Your spine
is lengthened and your abdominals are contracted. Your partner stands
behind you holding the middle of the band while you place your hands
through the handles of the band. Exhale and raise both arms straight up as
your standing partner adjusts the resistance of the band. Inhale and bring
both arms toward your partner (overhead), and then circle your arms out
to your sides (angel wings) and back to their starting position. Repeat this
exercise for 1–3 sets of 12–16 repetitions. Now it's time for your partner
to do the chest press exercise on the ball. You could choose to alternate
between sets so that each of you will get a rest in between.

one arm row with elastic band

Both partners should stand (or sit on stability balls) five feet apart, facing each other while holding an elastic band. Your partner will be sharing the opposite end of your band. Both of you hold onto the band in each hand with palms facing each other. Stand (or sit) up tall (meaning you have good posture and an extended spine) and contract your abdominals. Inhale and raise your arms straight in front of you. Exhale as you both press your arms back, with your elbows leading the movement (keep your elbows close to your body). Keep your shoulders relaxed and down. Repeat this exercise for 1–3 sets of 12–16 repetitions on each arm.

triceps extension with a towel or elastic band

One partner will get down on one knee holding an elastic band or twisted towel in one hand. The other partner will stand up tall, holding the opposite end with both hands. The kneeling partner will exhale and press the towel or band down toward the floor while extending through a full range of motion in the arm and squeezing the back of the arm (triceps). Keep the wrist in a neutral position during this exercise. Inhale and return to the starting position. Repeat this for 1–3 sets of 12–16 repetitions. Switch knees and arms, and repeat on the other side.

one-legged balancing biceps curl

Both partners should stand next to each other, each holding a dumbbell in her outside hand with palm facing forward. Keep your elbow close to your side. Place your inside arm up on your partner's shoulder and stand up tall, contracting your abdominal muscles. Each partner will bend her inside knee and lift it up to hip height. While balancing on one leg, exhale and lift your outside arm (the one with the weight) up to your chest and hold for a few seconds. Inhale and slowly lower the weight down to your side. Repeat this for 1–3 sets of 12–16 repetitions. Switch your position and repeat on the opposite arm. For a more advanced move, release your partner and curl both arms up to your chest at the same time.

One-Legged Balancing
Biceps Curl

Jump Squat and Throw

jump squat and throw

Both partners should stand facing each other about three to five feet apart. One partner will hold a medicine ball in front of her chest. Both partners will inhale and lower down into a squat position, keeping their knees back, abdominals contracted, and spines lengthened. Both partners will exhale and raise up to stand tall as the partner with the ball passes it directly in front of her chest and the other partner catches it. Both inhale, lower back down, and continue passing the ball for 12–16 repetitions and 1–3 sets. You can make this exercise advanced by jumping up in the air as you pass the ball.

standing torso twist with medicine ball

Stand back-to-back with your partner about three feet apart. Keep your hips facing forward and feet hip distance apart. Contract your abdominals and stand up tall. Exhale and pass the ball to one another by only rotating through your obliques (waist) and thoracic spine (middle back). Continue passing the ball in one direction for 10–16 repetitions. Pass the ball in the opposite direction for another set of 10–16 repetitions. Repeat again in the opposite direction.

Sit-up Pass

sit-up pass

Both of you lie on your backs, toe to toe, with knees bent while one partner holds a medicine ball in front of her chest. Engage your abdominal muscles. Exhale, and both partners lift your shoulders off the floor as one partner tosses the ball toward the other. Catch the ball and inhale as you return back to the floor, rolling down through your spine one vertebra at a time. Repeat this sit-up pass for 8–12 repetitions. Bring your knees into your chest and stretch the lower back between sets. Repeat this for 1–3 sets of 8–12 repetitions.

Shaped by God

The motivation and accountability of a fitness partner ensures that not only will we more easily reach our fitness goals, but we will also develop our relationships with others. Along those same lines, our spiritual development can be nurtured by joining up with a prayer partner.

Over the last few years, the Lord has sent many God-fearing women across my path. But one particular woman—who was hired as an instructor at the gym and who made her faith clear to me—became a very good friend. We quickly realized that not only were we compatible friends, but God had placed us in the same facility for His purposes. We became friends and prayer partners, and we still are today.

Once we recognized that God had brought us together for prayer, we took our prayer time together very seriously. To start, we placed a notebook on a table outside of the workout room along with a prayer box. The notebook is available for any of our students to write down their prayer requests for all to see. The small box is for private requests and stays closed. We read through the requests and pray for God's will in that person's life. Then we walk through the fitness facility, quietly praying over the workout facility, the equipment and the individual rooms. Our desire is that everyone who takes our fitness classes will experience the love of Christ and begin to draw close to Him.

The time we spend together in prayer is holy. Matthew 18 promises, "If two of you agree here on earth concerning anything you ask, my father in Heaven will do it for you. For where two or three gather together as my followers, I am there among them."

If you are interested in building a prayer partner relationship with someone, here are some things to consider. First, you must carefully choose your partner. Look for someone who already has a personal prayer life. Confidentiality is most important for private matters; make sure this person is trustworthy. If she is always talking about someone else's concerns, most likely she lacks maturity and would not be a good fit. Select someone who will share her own heart and personal experiences. Your partner should have a repentant spirit and a desire to live according to God's will.

You may have several good candidates in mind. Make a list of all the names that come to mind. Pray over the names, asking God to show you the right partner. Once God has revealed the person to you, call or meet with her to pray about the partnership. God does not make mistakes; He will lead you to pray with just the right person!

May God bless you with a great prayer partner and a stronger prayer life for His glory.

• ● •

Adopted into a Partnership with God

"As we emulate Christ's actions on the earth, we begin to become not only God's children but His partners in peace on this earth."

• ● •

God's Word in Romans 8:14–17 reminds us that when we invite Christ into our lives, we become His children: "For all who are led by the Spirit of God are children of God. So you should not be like cowering, fearful slaves. You should behave instead like God's very own children, adopted into His family— calling him "Father, dear Father." For his Holy Spirit speaks to us deep in our hearts and tells us that we are God's children. And since we are His children, we will share his treasures . . . .

So how do we apply this royal adoption to our own lives? We can start by behaving like royal heirs to the throne and choosing to live a life pleasing to God. As we emulate Christ's actions on earth, love flows easily from our hearts. Ever so naturally, we begin to become not only God's children but His partners in peace on this earth. We take on the active role of furthering His Gospel, and our identity as a child of God empowers us to move forward with strength and confidence. As God's heavenly child and earthly partner, we live with the assurance that this life is punctuated by an eternity spent with the "Abba Father," where we will join in the ultimate community in perfect union with God.

Shaped by Prayer

O GOD, MY GOD, I AM SO THANKFUL THAT YOU
ADOPTED ME INTO YOUR FAMILY. YOU ARE MY
FATHER AND REDEEMER. YOU RESCUED ME
WHEN LIFE SEEMED HOPELESS AND BLEAK.
I WILL PRAISE YOU ALL THE DAYS OF MY LIFE.
MAY MY LIFE BE A REFLECTION OF YOU AS I
GO OUT AMONG YOUR PEOPLE. HELP ME BE
APPROACHABLE, SO I MAY SHOW YOUR LOVE
TO EVERYONE. USE ME AS YOUR INSTRUMENT
IN MY HOME, WORKPLACE, AND WHEN
I EXERCISE. GUIDE AND DIRECT MY PATH,
FATHER, AND LEAD ME TO WHAT YOU HAVE
CALLED ME TO DO EACH AND EVERY DAY.
I LOVE YOU, FATHER.

Chapter Four

Stretch

> "ENLARGE THE PLACE OF YOUR TENT,
> STRETCH YOUR TENT CURTAINS WIDE,
> DO NOT HOLD BACK; LENGTHEN YOUR CORDS,
> STRENGTHEN YOUR STAKES."
>
> ISAIAH 54:2 (NIV)

As a child, sitting in the willow tree in my backyard gave me a new perspective of the world. If I followed the reach of its branches out far enough, I could see two streets over, where an ivy vine wrapped itself around my neighbors' gutter. I would sit there, safe in the arms of that strong tree, and think about the differences in the willow and the vine.

The willow had a thick trunk, ideal for climbing. Whether sunshine or rain, the willow offered a sanctuary from the weather conditions, all the while soothing my mind with its long flowing branches. The tree reminded me of a wise and gentle grandmother cradling me in her soft limbs. But the vine looked flimsy. She was pretty and green, but I knew that if I tried to climb the vine, I would instantly fall. The vine needed the gutter to wrap itself around, while my tree remained strong year-round. I remember wanting to be like that glorious willow. I wanted to be a comforting yet firm presence, someone whose reach was far, whose perspective was wide, and whose roots were deep.

Sadly, I have often lived more like the ivy vine, all tangled up in myself, stuck in the gutter. I was flimsy and depended on others, such as my father, for my own strength. But surprisingly, what has enabled me to more closely resemble the willow—stretched and not twisted—has been pain. Trials and challenges have caused me to widen my horizons, to learn how strong I am and to have solid roots, like the beautiful tree I admired so much.

When we stretch ourselves emotionally, physically and spiritually, we shake off our stiffness, our distorted selves, and open up to the world and the people around us. Stretching invigorates the body, mind, and soul. And with our limbs fully elongated, we can feel God's pleasure; we are the beauty of His creation.

Shaped by Life

Our wedding date was set for the end of July, scheduled to coincide with Brian's graduation from Air Force basic training. I had grand plans for our wedding day. I combed through stacks and stacks of bridal magazines. I imagined that my bridesmaids would wear elegant baby blue dresses and carry gorgeous bouquets of fresh lilies. My dress would be ivory with simple beading around the bodice and a long blue ribbon flowing down my back. Flowers would accent my hair in place of the traditional veil.

But my dreams would not come true. All the hours of studying and planning came to a halt when my father informed me that my wedding would be very small and simple, since I had disgraced the family by having a child out of wedlock. There would be no expensive ivory gown or bridesmaids with lilies. My sister Donna and a best man would be the only other participants in our wedding, and I would borrow a wedding dress from our neighbor. The wedding was in July, but the dress was long sleeved, meant for winter. A secondhand dress for a second-class bride.

As I slipped on the dress the morning of my wedding, I visualized my father looking at me and telling me I was beautiful. All the hurt feelings could have been forgotten if he had just told me how much he loved me and that I looked radiant.

Those words never came. Instead, he made his way to where I stood and said, "Let's get this show on the road."

The next morning, Brian had to catch a flight back to Wichita Falls, Texas, to continue his Air Force training. We made arrangements to reunite after he found an apartment close to the base. Christina kept me company while I waited on my new husband to find us a home.

A very long week went by until he finally called and said he had found a one-bedroom furnished apartment. A new home made me feel like I had the chance to start over—a new beginning in a new place. I remember holding Christina in my arms, speaking these words into her little ear, "You can do anything you set your mind to, and no matter what, I will be there to support you."

But life in Wichita Falls was different than I'd hoped. It was quiet and lonely. Brian would leave for training early in the morning, and I would sit home with my daughter all day. We had only one car, and he took it to school. There were no other military wives in our apartment complex. Soon, I was watching soap operas all day as I cared for Christina. My mother had not taught me to cook, so my dinners were limited to one of the following: breakfast food, fried rice or lasagna. After dinner, my husband and I would take our daughter for a walk. I looked forward to these short visits with him.

After a while, our peaceful times together grew more and more sporadic. Instead of walks, Brian began taking me to the Airman's Club on base, where other enlisted men would go to drink and unwind. But my presence there was a huge mistake, considering most of the men there were unmarried and there was a shortage of women on the base.

As Brian visited with his buddies, the other men would make suggestive and embarrassing comments to me. I would often feel threatened and uncomfortable, and I suggested we stay home on the weekends to avoid all these issues. Brian agreed, but then he began to invite his military buddies to the apartment. They would drink until the early hours of the morning. It became like the Airman's Club, except that it was in my home. This was not the life I wanted for my daughter. Our relationship essentially disintegrated during this time—I wanted to leave my husband but I didn't have a job to support Christina.

After a year in Wichita Falls, Brian was transferred to Offutt Air Force Base in Bellevue, Nebraska, and one-year-old Christina and I followed him there. We moved into an apartment complex, and things began to look up. There were several military couples at the complex, and most of them were very nice. It seemed that the majority of the young wives worked during the day to occupy their time. I felt like I was ready to take a job, so I began to work at a steakhouse.

The problem with working at the restaurant was that I was eating the food frequently, and eventually I had packed on an extra twenty-five pounds. For my frame, twenty-five pounds is a lot of weight to gain. Feeling burdened by the weight gain, I bought a gym membership. My daughter and I would catch rides with a girlfriend to the health club each day, and this is where I experienced my very first aerobic exercise class.

Theresa's Top Three for Stretching

1 Incorporate stretching into your daily routine. Take a few moments to stretch your back, neck and shoulders several times a day.

2 Reach out and help another person, even if it takes you out of your comfort zone.

3 Remember that hardships and trials that stretch you, while hard, bring you closer to God.

One of the things I learned quickly about my body was that it didn't respond particularly well to high-impact aerobics. That was especially true when I first joined the gym because I was so out of shape. I searched for an alternative class and found one called "dance thin." In dance thin, the instructor taught low-impact cardiovascular exercises and incorporated stretching and toning on the mat. Now *this* was my cup of tea. I loved mat work, especially stretching and abdominal exercises. I could actually get through the entire hour-long class without a side stitch, and I became quite flexible. For some reason, this class began to mean more to me than just a place to exercise—it made me feel like I had purpose, like I was growing. Not only did my body become flexible, it felt like my horizon was widening with brighter sunshine ahead.

Evidently, my passion for dance thin had become visible to the instructor. After I'd been in the class awhile, she asked if I would be interested in becoming certified to teach. She explained the process and said she thought I would make a good instructor. She went on to say she thought I would go far in this world. I wasn't sure if she meant the real world or the exercise world, but it didn't matter because she had my attention.

That was all I needed to start on the road to wellness. That little bit of encouragement filled me with excitement, and I became determined to be the best dance thin instructor in the whole world. I began teaching classes at the health club and then expanded my class schedule to include a few classes at the military base. Teaching gave me purpose and made me happy. It became my mission to inspire others to join me on this journey to physical wellness.

I now realize that during all these hardships—my father's continued disapproval and my husband's neglect—I was transitioning from a twisted ivy vine to a strong willow tree. My marriage was falling apart, and I was terribly lonely. Loneliness drove me to a seemingly random discovery of fitness, which became the lifeline I needed—and still need—to endure the process of becoming untangled.

Shaped by Fitness

Sometimes when times are hard, it seems that being stretched is more like medieval torture. Emotional stretching can be so painful, especially when it requires sacrifice and redirection. But I believe with all of my heart that when we are stretched beyond what we think we are capable of handling, God makes us stronger than ever before.

The same is true for physical stretching. We bring honor to God when we care for our physical bodies, and stretching—even though it can be hard, sometimes painful—is one of the most powerful tools we can use toward wellness. It increases our energy and overall range of motion, which reduces tension and stress and increases circulation. The more elongated we are, the better our bodies can function.

Flexibility training through dynamic stretching is essential to improving our overall health. Dynamic stretches combine momentum and muscles while increasing

● ● ●

"We bring honor to God when we care for our physical bodies, and the more elongated we are, the better our bodies can function."

● ● ●

body temperature and heart rate, and provide higher levels of oxygen to the muscles. Flexibility is required in most sports and aerobic activities, such as running, walking, cycling and swimming. We should also stretch before daily activities that require us to use large muscles such as heavy lifting, gardening, golfing, hiking and bowling.

And before a friendly game of basketball, softball, tennis or any sports-related activity, we should absolutely stretch. This is especially important for inactive people, who can suffer from extreme muscle soreness or even injury after impromptu activity. Most people who are sedentary do not think about the necessity of warming up the body and stretching before they start participating in higher impact activities.

So what is dynamic stretching? Dynamic stretching means customizing the muscles you stretch based on the activity you plan to do.

Suppose you are going to play a round of golf with a friend. Both of you should think about stretching your specific golfing muscles. If you don't know what these muscles are, stand in your golfing stance and take a few practice swings. Try feeling what muscles move when you swing, and base your stretches on those sensations. The key golfing muscles you should be noticing involve your abdominals, hamstrings, glutes, shoulders, and upper and lower back. Or suppose you are going on a long walk with a friend. Before you begin, walk a few steps, and, again, pay attention to the muscles that move.

One of the best ways to learn how to sense specific muscle movements is with Pilates. Pilates movements create an acute awareness of each muscle group in your body. Here are a few key Pilates exercises that help you stretch the majority of the muscles involved in activities like golf, walking and gardening. (By the way, did you know that you can burn up to four hundred calories per hour while digging, weeding, trimming shrubs, and mowing the lawn? The sport of gardening is a beautiful alternative to traditional exercise and a terrific way to enjoy the great outdoors.)

Before you get started, a few tips:

- Never bounce or jerk while stretching, because bouncing can cause injury.

- All stretches should be smooth and slow, allowing the muscle to extend through a full range of motion.

- Don't forget to breathe! Inhale and exhale before, during, and after a stretch. Deep, easy, even breathing is the key to releasing muscle tension and stress. Never hold your breath while you stretch.

PILATES SAW

Find a bench or ottoman and sit down. Sit with your legs extended in front of you, wider than hip width apart. Bend the knees slightly and contract your deep abdominal muscles as you focus on your breathing during the stretch. Lift both arms out to the side, shoulder height. Inhale and rotate your body to the right, keeping your bottom on the bench. Exhale and reach forward with your left hand past your right foot as you extend your right arm behind you. Inhale, roll back up, and return to center. Repeat this exercise on the other side. You can repeat this exercise up to 5–10 times on both sides. This exercise will dynamically warm up the hamstrings, spine and back, shoulder, abs, chest, and arm muscles.

Pilates Saw

GARDEN SQUAT

Because there is a lot of squatting and bending during activities like gardening (cleaning out a closet or attic involves similar movements), the squat is a perfect dynamic stretching exercise to complement this activity. While standing in the yard admiring the beauty of God's creation, prepare your body to squat by contracting the abdominal muscles and taking a deep inhale. Exhale and place your feet hip-width apart, keeping your back straight and your knees behind your toes. Inhale with your arms at your side, then lower down, sitting back over the heels. Hold this position through a breath cycle of one long exhale and inhale. To make the stretch slightly more intense, extend your arms out in front of your shoulders, parallel to the ground. Exhale and slowly stand back up to your starting position. Repeat the squat 8–12 times.

Whatever sport or activity you choose, remember to always stretch dynamically before engaging yourself in the exercise. Make sure you are stretching both sides of the body equally so that all of your muscles will be ready for action.

Stretching at Work

A few months ago, I had the pleasure of preparing a stretching video for a corporation that wanted to decrease the number of injuries in their workplace. The job required employees to lift heavy pipes and equipment while working outside in drainage ditches.

I was proud to be a part of creating this video and was inspired by the conscientious human resource director who knew the importance of incorporating stretches into the workplace. Whether you work in a physically demanding environment or at a desk, adding flexibility exercises to your daily routine will not only make you more productive, but will also greatly reduce soreness and potential for injury.

Here are several stretches that are specifically tailored for a work environment. On days when you feel really motivated, feel free to do each exercise. Otherwise, you may want to do one exercise per day, rotating stretches from day to day, week to week.

UPPER BACK STRETCH

Inhale and stand or sit straight, maintaining good posture, with your knees slightly bent. Place your feet hip-distance apart. With your palms facing forward, exhale and extend both arms in front of you as far as you can reach with one palm resting on the top of the opposite hand. Make sure to keep your shoulders down, away from your ears. Hold this stretch for 15–30 seconds as you feel the stretch in your upper back. Repeat up to five times.

LOWER BACK STRETCH

Stand or sit with your feet shoulder-width apart. Contract your abdominals. Inhale as you bend forward at the hips, resting your hands on your thighs. Tuck your chin in toward your chest as you round (flex) your back (spine) toward the ceiling, keeping your shoulders down, feeling mild tension through the back. Hold this stretch for 15–30 seconds. Release; then lift up your head and reverse the arch in your back. Hold for 15–30 seconds. Repeat this stretch pattern up to five times. Don't forget to breathe through the stretch!

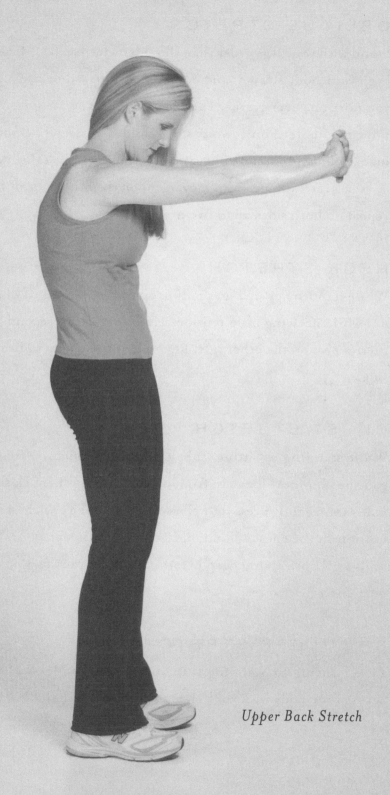

Upper Back Stretch

OBLIQUE STRETCH

Stand with your legs wider than shoulder width apart. Make sure that you keep your body straight and do not lean forward or backward. Inhale as you raise one arm overhead and lean to the opposite side. You will notice mild muscle tension in your side. Hold this stretch as you breathe and focus your attention on the stretched muscles—in other words, breathe *into* the stretch. Repeat this movement on the other side of your body, and repeat on both sides up to five times.

NECK STRETCH

While standing or sitting, slowly drop your ear down to your right shoulder while noticing mild tension. Hold for fifteen seconds. Release, and then repeat on the other side. Repeat this stretch up to five times on each side.

CHEST STRETCH

While standing or sitting, inhale and place touching fingertips behind your head. Move elbows in front of you, placing them close together. Exhale as you gently press your elbows back to open the chest, noticing mild tension in the chest and middle back. Hold this position for 15–30 seconds while practicing deep breathing. Return to start position, and repeat up to five times.

SHOULDER STRETCH

Either sitting or standing with your feet shoulder-width apart, reach across your body with your right arm, your left hand holding your right arm just above your elbow. Exhale as you press your right arm closer in to your body, feeling mild tension in the shoulder. Make sure your shoulders are pressed down away from your ears during this stretch. Hold the stretch for 15–30 seconds. Repeat the shoulder stretch on the opposite arm.

ELASTICITY

Flexibility is one thing, and elasticity is quite another. There's a certain weightlessness and increased reflexivity that comes from being elastic. But transcending flexibility into elasticity requires more than simple stretches; it requires the kind of stretching that makes you sweat, and it often feels painful. If you've participated in Pilates, you know what I mean. Incidentally, the best tools I've found for increasing elasticity are elastic bands.

Elastic bands will add even more intentionality to a stretching program, because they allow you to increase resistance only as you become more and more flexible. Working with the stretch bands increases our muscle strength and stability, while toning and stretching our muscles at the same time. Before you know it, these bands will have you feeling truly elastic.

Physical therapists were the first group of people to use stretch bands to help people regain their strength and flexibility after an injury or surgery. Now, resistance bands are available to everyone in the privacy of their own home. There is no pressure placed on the joints while using the resistance bands or tubing. They are versatile and do not take up much space, so you can take them anywhere you go, even traveling or on vacation.

To get started using the stretch bands, begin with the lowest resistance bands first. Make sure you bring awareness to your breath as you use controlled movements and allow the resistance of the exercise bands to stretch and strengthen your muscles in the following three exercises listed. Remember, these are not easy stretches—that's why it's key to breathe into them and increase resistance only when you're comfortable with the lighter bands first.

PILATES LEG CIRCLE WITH STRETCH BAND

Begin by lying supine (on your back) with one leg extended toward the ceiling and the other leg flat on the mat. Place the band around your raised foot and hold the ends of the band tightly with both hands. Exhale as you extend your leg straight—as straight as you can make it, while still keeping a neutral spine and your opposite leg stable and anchored to the mat. Inhale as you begin to circle the extended leg and exhale as you complete the circle back to your starting position. Repeat this leg circle five times in one direction and then five times going the opposite direction. You should be able to feel the stretch in your thighs as it increases your core and hip stability at the same time.

For the novice stretcher, bend the leg that rests on the mat so that your foot is flat on the floor. Then, bend your extended leg. Repeat this exercise three times in one direction and three times in the opposite direction.

For the advanced exercise enthusiast, you can increase the size of the circle so that the leg crosses over the body and is low to the floor. Be sure to do this without compromising your spine and core stability.

Hamstring Stretch

HAMSTRING STRETCH

Lie on the floor supine and place the band around your right foot while holding one end of the band in each hand to create tension. Inhale as you slowly straighten your right leg, keeping your left leg either flat against the mat or bent. Exhale and gently pull your leg toward your chest until you notice tension in the back of your leg. Hold this stretch for 15–30 seconds; then switch legs. Repeat this stretch on each leg 3–5 times.

Start by lying on the floor supine, place the band around your right foot, and hold the ends of the band in your left (opposite) hand. Bend or straighten your left leg out on the floor and exhale as you lower your right leg across your body and to your left side as low as you can go, feeling the stretch in the right hip and glute. Breathe! Hold for 15–30 seconds and switch to the opposite leg. Repeat this stretch on each leg 3–5 times.

Shaped by God

There have been numerous times when I have been forced into an uncomfortable situation. One particular event stands out in my memory as something that really forced me out of my comfort zone and into what I call the "faith zone."

Fast-forward several years, I had four children, and our financial situation was dire. I was working four different jobs to make ends meet. Yes, *four* jobs, and still, we had no extra money to spend after paying the rent, car insurance and utility bills. My first job each day was working at the YMCA as a fitness instructor. One day, while leaving the Y to go home and get ready for my next job as a receptionist, I heard God speak to my heart.

There was a lady I worked with at the Y who was always kind to my children and me. Pearl knew we were struggling financially, and she kept my kids in the nursery while I taught classes. As I walked past Pearl's desk, I felt God ask me to give her the only twenty-dollar bill in my purse, the one that had to last until the next payday, still several days away. I continued walking, thinking that the voice I heard was just my imagination. After all, why would God want me to give all the money that I had to someone else when I needed it to buy diapers? As I got in my car, I asked God to show me a sign if it really was His idea. I headed out of the parking lot, and I decided that I would give her money when I got paid in a few days.

But before I made it to the exit, I saw Pearl walking toward her car. I stared at her for a moment, taking her presence as a sign from God. I reparked my old beat-up car, grabbed my twenty-dollar bill, and started running toward her.

She turned toward me, confused. I handed her the bill, telling her that God wanted her to have this money. As she unfolded the twenty, tears began streaming down her face. She explained that it was the exact amount she needed to pay a past-due bill. Pearl thanked me with a heartfelt hug, and I walked back to my car.

"I have learned to appreciate the way God stretches our perspective of the world. He takes us beyond our comfort zones and rewards us for being obedient to Him."

As I drove home, I thanked God for allowing me to be used by Him. Even though I didn't have a lot, He used all I had for His glory. Rounding a curve, I saw our home, and I knew deep within my heart that God would supply our needs over the next few days, though I just didn't know how.

When I got home, there was a mysterious package on the back porch—it was full of diapers! The next morning,

I opened the front door and noticed something attached to my driver's side window. I couldn't believe it—there was a twenty-dollar bill somehow attached to my window without anything securing it. Without grabbing the bill, I ran back inside the house and got my children to show them the twenty-dollar bill on our car window. They were so happy and excited, and I told them that God must have asked one of His angels to hold it in place until I found it.

That incident was monumentally stretching for me. Yes, it threatened to stretch my finances—but what really changed was my appreciation for the way God stretches our perspective of the world. He takes us beyond our comfort zones and rewards us for being obedient to Him.

God continues to reward my family and me beyond comprehension. What used to be uncomfortable for me has now become a blessing, just as physical stretching was once painful but is now second nature. Every day, I become increasingly limber in body and soul. And like the willow tree I looked up to as a child, I reach for the sky with grace and praise.

Shaped by Prayer

LORD, MY PRAYER TODAY IS THAT I
WOULD GROW STRONGER IN MY FAITH
AS I STRETCH MY ARMS OUT
IN SERVICE TO YOU. HELP ME TO BE AN
EXTENSION OF YOU AS I REACH OUT TO
OTHERS. STRENGTHEN MY WEAK LIMBS AND
EQUIP ME WITH YOUR SWORD OF TRUTH.
YOU ARE THE VINE, AND I AM ONE OF YOUR
BRANCHES; MAY I HONOR YOU IN ALL THAT
I DO TODAY. IN THE NAME OF JESUS I PRAY,
AMEN.

Align

In modeling, grace is the product of correct alignment. When demonstrated properly, the model is expected to maintain perfect posture with her chin held up and her eyes focused straight ahead. Just to make it interesting, this is all done in the highest of high heels.

As a student at the Nancy Bounds School of Modeling, I knew that if I were less than perfectly aligned, I would be harshly corrected by Nancy herself. Every model knew: Nancy was the picture of grace, and she expected us to be, too.

One day, as I descended the studio's concrete steps after a long practice session, I lost focus momentarily and drooped my posture. Because

I had spent the day in such perfect alignment, the adjustment somehow shocked my body. I tumbled down the stairs, ending my fall with a bloodied leg and shredded pantyhose. My first act, after coming to a stop, was not to check my body for injuries, but to look behind me to see if Nancy had seen me fall. She hadn't, and I was relieved. But I realize now that Nancy's obsession with alignment was a positive lesson to learn and translates beyond modeling. After all, if our bodies and spirits aren't in line, we fall out of step.

Shaped by Life

I had been teaching dance thin for about a year and was still at Offutt AFB with Brian when I decided to attend modeling school. I was a mom of two now, but I found that I really enjoyed modeling and was eventually promoted from student to modeling instructor at Nancy's studio. I had the pleasure of coaching and training several young ladies who wound up on the covers of *Seventeen, ELLE, Mademoiselle,* and several other respected magazines. My students' successes felt like my success; I had taught them well.

But one of the things I liked most about teaching at the studio was that I worked under Nancy's mentorship. Even though I was the youngest instructor on staff, Nancy looked on me with favor and mentored me privately. Nancy instilled in me a mind-set that I could conquer the world if I truly believed in myself.

Knowing that she believed in me motivated me to savor every morsel of information about the modeling industry. After all, even though I loved teaching, my dreams of being in the limelight myself were hardly diminished.

Nancy's step-by-step instructions were like a recipe to success. She emphasized the value of presenting yourself to the public in a confident manner, even when you did not feel confident on the inside. Nancy showed me how to enter a room with grace and style; then she demonstrated how to grab the attention of everyone in the room without saying a word. While studying, I was in absolute awe of her ability to glide gracefully with confidence and style while wearing high heels. Nancy never spoke of her age, but she had to be in her late fifties.

One of the most valuable things Nancy taught me was proper posture. She was a petite lady, but I do not think there was a person who ever thought of her as small. Her posture was consistently extended up, her head level and her eyes focused straight ahead. She expected me never to look at the floor while standing or walking. She also said that the best way to think about good posture was to be able to glide across the floor in high heels or descend a staircase better than Cinderella ever dreamed. All of this while keeping my eyes level, spine and head reaching upward, toward the ceiling. Another important process that I still practice today is scooping the belly to the spine, from morning to night. By implementing these fundamentals, I would be able to demonstrate to the world a polished product of Nancy Bounds International. I had not only learned to align my posture, but I had also learned how to align myself to a practice—a path toward success. And I felt proud of that.

While I was working at the studio, my friend and co-instructor Cindy and I were chosen to take a group of our students to a national modeling convention in Kansas City, Missouri. Upon our arrival at the convention, we signed the ladies up for several different modeling divisions, such as runway, commercial, talent, and photography. Cindy suggested that I sign myself up for the commercial competition. At first I was hesitant, knowing that I needed to help the other girls practice and perfect their runway walk. But with her continued encouragement—and after reminding myself that being center stage was my dream too—I signed up.

One of my most vivid memories of the convention was the commercial competition. In it, I had to get on a platform and deliver lines that were handed to me just minutes before I took the stage. I remember that the commercial was about panty hose. The judges praised me for my delivery of the lines and said I would do very well in television. When it was time for callbacks, my number was called, and I walked over with poise—thanks to Nancy—to meet the owner of Tracey's Agency out of New York.

The agent's conversation with me was curt and to the point. She said I would do well on a sitcom or a soap opera. In order for any of this to become a reality, though, I would need to move to New York. Once there, I could begin my work in commercials while she lined up auditions for sitcoms and soap operas. She would provide an apartment and commercial opportunities to become established. When I mentioned that I had two young daughters (Candice had been born less than a year before), her eyes cut across the table as she said, "New York is no place to bring children when pursuing a television career. You will have to leave them behind for a while until you are on a sitcom or soap opera."

But who would care for my girls? At that point, my marriage had all but fallen apart.

One evening, Brian told me point-blank that he was divorcing me, and I called Cindy for comfort. Cindy was ten years older than me, and I trusted her advice. Cindy was divorced, had three sons, and lived in Omaha. She told me that she had been trying to find another place to live in Omaha, because her one-bedroom apartment was not big enough to support her three children, who were currently living with her ex-husband. Eventually, the discussion turned into a plan: Cindy would find a big house in Omaha that we could share. As I hung up the phone, the dark realization set in that my marriage was over, and that my girls and I would be moving from Bellevue, Nebraska, to Omaha with my friend and her children.

Theresa's Top Three for Alignment

1 Scoop your belly. By pulling your belly button to your spine, you will be strengthening your back and abdominal muscles all day long.

2 Keep focused on what is truly important to you, whatever that may be. Let other tasks and responsibilities fall into place around that priority.

3 Practice proper posture. Gradually correcting your posture will not only give you a confident stance, it will improve your overall health.

But I certainly couldn't ask Cindy to take care of my children and her own while I pursued my television career in New York—Christina was only four at the time, and Candice was nine months old. So I went to the only other person I could think of: my father.

I knew exactly how my father felt about my dreams. He believed I should get a "real job" like my sister, who was a schoolteacher. But, out of desperation, I thought that just maybe he might agree to watch Christina and Candice for six months while I gave acting a try in New York. I tried to reason with him; if I could make it in New York, I would have plenty of money to raise the girls. My father simply reminded me that my daughters were my responsibility and he was not going to raise them.

In the short time that I had been mentored by Nancy, I had learned so much about grace, poise, and alignment. But she taught me about more than just physical beauty. I was always amazed by how Nancy handled difficult situations in her life. She would remind me to always stand tall regardless of the circumstances that challenged me. Nancy's wise words flooded back to me as I debated whether to go to New York. I knew that if I tried hard enough, I could find a way to keep my girls safe and try to make it in television. But at what cost? Would I be standing tall or would I crumble under the pressure? And even more importantly, what would I be standing tall *for*?

Eventually, I made the call to the agent in New York. I turned her offer down. She said that she understood why, but told me I was missing the opportunity of a lifetime. I mourned for that dream, but I loved my daughters more than my career.

Shaped by Fitness

I am always surprised when I see athletes or fellow instructors who totally disregard their own posture. I remember on one occasion actually being lectured against demonstrating perfect posture while teaching step classes. My supervisor tried to convince me that people only wanted a workout and not a class on posture—I felt like I was on a different planet.

Twenty-five years later, I still remind each of my students in every class to maintain their posture during cardio, strength training, and flexibility exercises. Without good posture and body alignment, our muscles and bones are at a high risk for injury. Among many benefits of good posture is relief from pain in the back, neck, hips and legs, which allows us to move more efficiently.

Here are a couple of alignment exercises to help your posture. They will also help you demonstrate confidence.

COMBINED ALIGNMENT AND ABDOMINAL EXERCISE

Stand up tall with your shoulders pulled back. Gently scoop your belly button toward your spine while sitting or standing (it feels as if you're hollowing out your belly). Take a deep inhale to prepare and exhale as you scoop. Remember to keep your spine lengthened. Hold for a few minutes and then repeat. Do the belly scoop everywhere you go—shopping, walking, driving, talking on your phone, working—eventually, it will become second nature. Scooping your belly toward your spine will significantly improve your alignment, and it will also strengthen and support your lower back (lumbar) muscles.

POSTURE EXERCISE

Begin correcting your posture while standing.

- Set your feet and legs directly under your hips. Your knees should be straight, but not locked.

- Gently rock back and forth on your feet until you feel that your body weight is evenly distributed over the center of your foot.

- Engage your abdominals (scoop your belly) by pulling them in and then up toward your sternum.

- Drop your tailbone directly toward the floor. (Imagine that your pelvis is a bowl of water you don't want to spill, which will help you find a natural curve in the spine.)

- Open up your chest and expand your back.

- Drop your shoulders away from your ears and allow your shoulder blades to glide down your back.

- Keep your head and neck in a neutral position with your spine. Your eyes should be looking forward with your chin resting naturally.

Unlike other exercises with limited repetitions, proper posture should be practiced twenty-four hours a day. I know that seems hard, but just start slow. Begin practicing good posture as you cook a meal; then try it while you sit at your desk. After a while, you'll think about your posture more often, which will make good posture a more natural feeling.

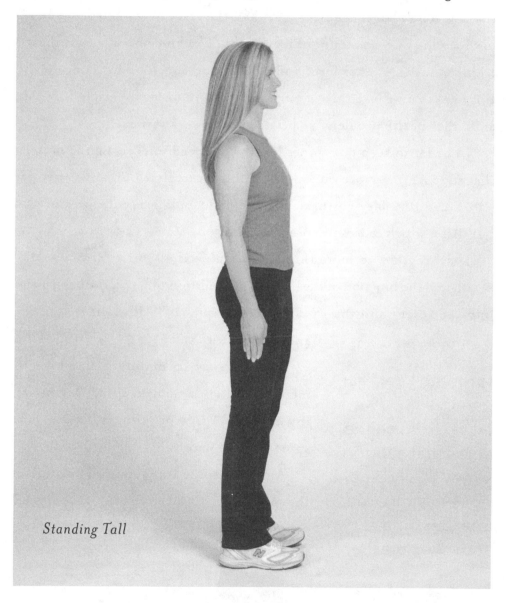

Standing Tall

Spine Alignment

Our spines are so wonderfully unique. The spine is one of the few structures of the body that provide both stability and mobility. It is the structural foundation of the body. It is composed of thirty-three bones called vertebrae, and our lower back (lumbar spine) is composed of five bones that are much larger and stronger than the rest of the vertebrae and allow for the greatest amount of movement. The lower back muscles bear a tremendous amount of force and still support much of our body weight. It is vital that we take care of our lower back in order to lessen back pain and other health problems associated with a weak spine.

In order to keep our spines healthy, we need to exercise the muscles that support and move our spine. Without exercise, our spines become stiff and inflexible. Postural misalignment puts excessive pressure on our discs, which causes intense pain.

Learning how to move through the spine is essential for our overall health and the function of the body. The condition of our spine has a major impact on everything that we do. When the spine is healthy, life feels better, and we move with ease.

• ● •

"In order to keep our spines healthy, we need to exercise the muscles that support and move our spine. Without exercise, our spines become stiff and inflexible."

• ● •

The best way to maintain spine alignment is through a neutral spine. Maintaining a neutral spine position will allow your spine to move naturally.

A neutral spine is the natural position of the spine when all three curves of the spine—cervical (neck), thoracic (middle), and lumbar (lower)—are in proper alignment.

In order to find your neutral spine position, lie down on your back and bend your knees with your feet flat on the floor. Next, contract your core muscles by scooping your belly button toward your spine. You will notice that your lower back is comfortable with a neutral curve. By engaging your abdominals you should be able to maintain this neutral spine position while the core muscles help protect and stabilize the spine. It is important that you practice and maintain a neutral spine at all times, or at least as often as possible.

Here are a few exercises that will help strengthen and challenge your alignment. Remember to maintain a neutral spine while moving through each of these exercises.

SEATED SPINE TWIST (FOR SPINE FLEXIBILITY)

Begin by sitting on the floor with both legs extended straight out in front of you, with your feet together and flexed. Reach both of your arms out to the sides, shoulder height.

Inhale and elongate the spine and chest while keeping both shoulders down and back with the abdominal muscles contracted. Exhale and rotate the body (through the middle back) to one side without bending over, moving from the spine without any movement in the the spine twist on the other side. You can repeat this entire sequence for 3–5 repetitions on each side.

If your hamstrings and hip flexors feel too tight, cross your legs in front of your body.

Seated Spine Twist

SINGLE LEG STRETCH
(FOR SPINE STABILIZATION)

Lie down on your back with your left leg straight on the floor and your right leg raised to your chest. Place your right hand on your right shin or beside your right ankle. Place your left hand on the inside of your right knee. Raise your left leg a few inches off the floor. Flex your spine as you lift your shoulders and upper back off the floor and look toward your belly. Keep your core muscles engaged as you exhale; then switch legs and corresponding hand positioning. Inhale and switch again. Continue switching legs and keeping your core stabilized through this exercise. Do not move through your back or spine; only move your legs and arms. Repeat ten times on each leg.

For a modified stretch, raise your extended leg toward the ceiling and keep your upper body on the floor. For an advanced version, increase the speed of the exercise without sacrificing postural alignment and control.

Single Leg Stretch

Swim Simulation

SWIM SIMULATION (STRENGTHENS THE MUSCLES ALONG THE SPINAL COLUMN)

Lie on the floor in a prone position (belly down) with your head and neck in alignment with your spine. Lengthen your hips and legs; then reach your arms and legs off the floor. Extend your arms overhead in line with your ears (shoulder width apart) as you lengthen your legs straight back. Engage your abdominal muscles and reach further through your arms and legs. Inhale and lift your head off the floor, looking straight down. Raise one arm and the opposite leg higher while reaching them further away from your body. Exhale and lower your arm and leg, keeping them off the floor. Inhale and raise your other arm and leg, repeating the same lowering and lifting movement. Switch your legs and arms every count as you create a fluttering quality of movement. Continue the swim exercise for 3–5 sets of ten repetitions.

Shaped by God

Calamities befall everyone. For some people, minor incidents can send them reeling. For others, an impossible situation, one seemingly worthy of total self-absorption, does not cause them to raise an eyebrow. What's the difference? More than likely, the person who is standing tall in the storm has discovered spiritual alignment.

Now that I am a Christian, Nancy's simple but profound advice about standing tall translates into one of the creeds I rely on today: "I can stand tall by aligning myself to my Lord and Savior, Jesus Christ." Although I wasn't a follower of Christ when I made my decision against New York, I know now that He was there, protecting me, helping me stand tall, even when I didn't know I could.

The principles about figuratively standing tall have influenced the way I view the principles of physical posture and proper alignment. I know that aligning myself with Christ is essential to standing tall against hardship and for His Gospel, just as building strong posture allows me to literally stand tall, which, of course, promotes optimum fitness.

Nancy's strong persona was a living example of how to put on a mask of confidence no matter the circumstances, no matter the situation. While my world was crumbling around me, this mask allowed me to appear as though I had the world by the tail. It was an effective tool for working the runway or social gatherings . . . but when it came to real life, I needed something more; I needed a spiritual backbone to support me.

Scripture is full of resources for standing tall in God. My favorite passage is found in Ephesians 6:10–18. Paul tells us, "Finally, my brethren, be strong in the Lord and in the power of His might. Put on the whole armor of God, that you may be able to stand against the wiles of the devil. For we do not wrestle against

> **"I can stand tall by aligning myself to my Lord and Savior, Jesus Christ."**

"Interestingly, Paul never mentions the back—perhaps because each element of God's armor completely supports the spine—which spiritually speaking, is our relationship with Christ."

flesh and blood, but against principalities, against powers, against the rulers of the darkness of this age, against spiritual hosts of wickedness in the heavenly places. Therefore take up the whole armor of God, that you may be able to withstand in the evil day, and having done all, to stand. Stand therefore, having girded your waist with truth, having put on the breastplate of righteousness, and having shod your feet with the preparation of the gospel of peace; above all, taking the shield of faith with which you will be able to quench all the fiery darts of the wicked one. And take the helmet of salvation, and the sword of the Spirit, which is the Word of God; praying always with all prayer and supplication in the Spirit, being watchful to this end with all perseverance and supplication for all the saints" (NKJV).

Paul tells the Ephesians to put on the whole armor, leaving nothing at risk. Temptation and frustration stand peering around the corner, waiting for us to become distracted and out of alignment. When everyday life, calamity, or spiritual darkness has me slumping, I put on His armor and I can stand tall. His breastplate protects my vitals, including my heart. His girdle of truth protects my core and strengthens me. The helmet of salvation shields my head and allows my mind to hear His truth. My feet are covered so I may walk His walk and carry His message. And I carry the sword of faith to ward off discouragement. Interestingly, Paul never mentions the back—perhaps because each element of God's armor completely supports the spine—which, spiritually speaking, is our relationship with Christ. With the armor on, standing tall becomes second nature.

Spiritual alignment requires one decision: Will you put on His whole armor? Just as aligning our physical spine makes us strong, balanced, and healthy, aligning ourselves with God and putting on His armor strengthens us, protects us, and satisfies our soul.

Shaped by Prayer

YOU ARE THE KING OF KINGS AND THE LORD
OF LORDS; YOUR MERCY EXTENDS FOREVER
AND EVER. I WILL PRAISE YOU ALL THE DAYS
OF MY LIFE. PLEASE FORGIVE ME, FATHER,
WHEN MY SPIRITUAL POSTURE DOES NOT LINE
UP WITH YOUR WORD. HELP ME TO STAND
TALL AND STRONG BEFORE MEN AS
I REPRESENT YOU. LORD, I ALSO NEED YOUR
STRENGTH TO HELP ME WITH MY PHYSICAL
POSTURE. REMIND ME TO STAY LENGTHENED
IN MY SPIRITUAL AND PHYSICAL POSTURE ALL
DAY LONG AND INTO THE EVENING. MAY ALL
WHO SEE ME KNOW THAT YOU ARE
THE REASON MY BODY STANDS UPRIGHT.
I PRAY THESE THINGS THROUGH YOUR
HOLY NAME. AMEN.

Transform

The tadpole's metamorphosis into a frog is one of folklore's most beloved metaphors for transformation. But for me, it's a particularly profound image.

Like most kids, I trudged my way from childhood into dreaded adolescence. Above all else, my physical change was most apparent, but also notable were changes in my behavior and confidence. As my adolescence came to completion, I became a young woman and my confidence soared. My legs were twice as long as my trunk, my face gained a womanly fairness, and I became quite athletic. One of my favorite things to do during my early teen years was jump over full-sized metal trashcans. Many of my male counterparts were impressed by (and jealous of) my athleticism, and gave me the nickname Frog. I was just another tadpole who had been transformed.

Transformation is one of those processes we must endure. Just as our lives are changed as we go through adolescence, and just as our hearts are changed as we grow in maturity with the Lord, our fitness journeys must bring transformation in our bodies. For fitness to be at its best, we must progress, change, and grow. We start as physical tadpoles—listening to our bodies and growing in strength—and we slowly transform into fully capable frogs, transcendent of the form we once knew.

Theresa's Top Three for
Transformation

1 Turn your home into your own private fitness center by using ordinary things you already have, like laundry detergent and a kitchen chair.

2 To grow both our physical and spiritual bodies, we must be committed to working toward transformation, knowing that it is a process that will take time.

3 Do not conform to the patterns and wisdom of this world, but be transformed by Christ's spirit.

Shaped by Life

In dozens of years as a fitness instructor, I have met many, many people. But few have meant as much to me as Susie.

Susie was a student at the facility I worked at in Owensboro, where I had recently moved. At the time, I felt and acted very shielded. My divorce from Brian was final, and, in what I now consider to be one of the biggest mistakes of my life, I was newly married to a man I had met in Omaha. I married my second husband because I was lonely, desperate for money, and he had promised me the world. What I got instead was a man who was unable to care for me, my finances, my children . . . or himself.

Sad and bitter, I didn't trust many people. I refused to let anyone in, and it showed. People stayed away from me, and I took comfort in that fact. I wanted to be left alone.

But one day, Susie approached me after class, breaking my invisible "do-not-cross" barrier. She began the conversation point-blank by telling me that she was a Christian. Something about her loving spirit captured me—her eyes were bright and vibrant. It was as if they were shining light as she spoke about her love for Jesus Christ.

Susie's confidence and boldness were different from anything I had seen before. There was something special about this woman, and I wanted to hear more of what she had to say. "Jesus wants you to know that He loves you and wants to heal you," she said. I was not following.

She then asked a question that nearly knocked me over.

"Do you have a bleeding disorder?" she asked, and said that the Lord had revealed it to her during class.

My first reaction was that she wasn't right in the head, which would perhaps explain why she was so gentle—she was nuts. Or, perhaps she was on strong medication.

But how could she be crazy if her assessment was true? About three years prior to that day, I had given birth to my daughter Candice, and I had been bleeding nonstop ever since. I'd seen a physician, who told me that I had endometriosis, and that I would need a hysterectomy to cure it before things got out of control. In fact, I was scheduled for the hysterectomy within that month.

Since I was not a Christian at the time, I felt a little weird and embarrassed by Susie's confidence in God. I didn't know how to respond. There were several other ladies in the room, chatting with one another, and I became fearful that they might overhear our conversation. I didn't want the others to think I was crazy like Susie, so I thanked her for sharing her thoughts and excused myself to pick up Candice at preschool. Susie gave me a heartfelt smile and said she would be praying for me. I thanked her and quickly exited the building.

Later that day, I put my daughter down for a nap and began to clean the house, mopping our dirty entryway with the door open. As I turned toward the door, there was Susie! I wondered how she knew where I lived, since we had just moved in, but I welcomed her into our home anyway. Susie did not dance around subjects; immediately, she asked if she could pray with me. She told me she felt compelled to obey God by praying for my healing. With no one in sight and Candice napping, I told her that would be nice.

Both of her hands reached out for mine, and I hesitated. Why was she reaching for my hands? If she was so in touch with other things about me, why couldn't she sense that I wasn't a touchy-feely kind of person?

But the moment she held my hands, a peace fell upon me that was beyond my comprehension. My blood felt warm as a rush of energy went from my head down to my toes. In her short, simple prayer, she asked Jesus to come into my life and heal my endometriosis.

As I walked Susie to the door that day, I felt on fire. Did God really care about me and what was going on inside my body? I couldn't imagine someone loving me that much. I closed the door and fell to my knees. I didn't know how to pray or even how to speak to God, so I spoke to Him like I would anyone else.

I said, "God if you are real, please help me. I need you."

I continued, out loud, with words that seemed a mix of Susie's prayer and some kind of spiritual instinct. "I believe that Jesus Christ is the Son of God, that He was crucified and died, and on the third day rose again to save me." I wept and asked Him to take control of my life.

Just then, I felt all my guilt fall off my shoulders. I felt free for the first time, loved by Someone I couldn't even see. I wanted to know more, and I knew I had to read the Bible and see what God had to say.

What I realized in that moment was that God had always been there; I was just blind to it. That knowledge made me praise Him even more for His great love for me.

The next week, before one of my aerobics classes began, Susie asked me, "Well, are you healed?" Honestly, I had not given a thought to my bleeding. But as I paused to think about it, I realized the bleeding stopped the day Susie came over. I had been so focused on reading God's Word and incorporating prayer into my daily routine that I totally forgot about the blood.

I shared with Susie that the bleeding had stopped, and she began to praise God out loud. In front of everyone in the room, she started waving her arms up high and dancing around. Sure, I was a little self-conscious, but even still, her joy was my own.

Shaped by Fitness

Deciding to allow God full access to my heart was only the first step. After inviting Him into my life, I wanted to know more about Him and started ravenously devouring His Word. Our experience with exercise often feels similar. Of course, our desire for God always comes first, but once we discover the way exercise makes us feel, the way it improves our lives, we can't get enough.

But just like our lives of faith, effective exercise means transformation. It means growth and improvement. We should always challenge our bodies by progressing our workouts so that we can become even stronger.

There are a variety of ways we can progress as we exercise. We can choose to change the speed of an exercise. Or we can increase weight, intensity and repetitions. We can also add balance or position our bodies differently while working out.

I am always looking for new ways to

> "Just like our lives of faith, effective exercise means transformation. It means growth and improvement."

change a traditional exercise so that my body does not get used to it. My muscles and mind are pleasantly surprised when I change the look or intensity of an exercise; they have to work more intentionally to achieve what I am asking them to do.

Here are a few traditional exercises paired with progressions that I use in my workout routines. Take these exercises at your own pace and remember to maintain good posture through each exercise. If you find that good posture is too hard to maintain in the progression, then stay with the traditional form of the exercise for six weeks and try the progression again.

UPPER BODY

TRADITIONAL: KNEE PUSH-UP (CHEST)

Start on all fours with your hands a bit wider than your shoulders. Walk your knees back in order to lean your weight on your hands and straighten your back. Exhale and contract your abdominals as you bend your elbows and lower your body toward the floor until your elbows are at a ninety-degree angle. Inhale and hold for a second, and then exhale as you push back up. Repeat for 1–3 sets of 12–16 repetitions.

PROGRESSION: PUSH-UP ON THE BALL

Kneel on the floor with the ball in front of you and roll forward, walking your hands out to where you can support your body by pulling your abs in. Keep your shoulders down and your spine straight. Place your hands wider than your shoulders. Inhale and bend your elbows as you lower down to the floor with your elbows at a ninety-degree angle. Exhale and push back up to your starting position. Repeat this exercise for 1–3 sets of 12–16 repetitions.

Push-up on the Ball

TRADITIONAL: FRONT RAISE (SHOULDERS)

Hold a set of light or medium weights or soup cans with your arms straight down and palms facing your legs. Exhale and slowly lift your arms up to shoulder height while keeping your elbows slightly bent. Hold for a second, and inhale as you lower your arms back down. Repeat this exercise for 1–3 sets of 12–16 repetitions.

Front Raise and Tilt

PROGRESSION: FRONT RAISE AND TILT

Start by balancing on one leg as you contract your abdominals and hold a set of weights straight down with your palms facing your legs. Exhale and slowly lift your arms up to shoulder height, keeping your elbows slightly bent. Hold this position, and then tilt the weights in toward one another and then back. Tilt four times and then lower the weights back down as you inhale. Repeat this for 1–3 sets of 12–16 repetitions. Balance on the opposite leg after each set.

LOWER BODY

TRADITIONAL: BALL SQUAT

Stand with your feet hip-width apart and place an exercise ball behind your lower back and against the wall. Keep your arms straight down at your sides or place your hands on your hips. Inhale and bend your knees and lower into a squat, keeping your knees behind your toes. Lower down as far as you can go, and then exhale and push into the heels to go back up. Repeat this for 1–3 sets of 12–16 repetitions.

PROGRESSION: MOVING WEIGHTED SQUAT

Stand up tall with your feet hip width apart. Hold medium to heavy weights in each hand with arms bent above your shoulders. Inhale and bend your knees as you lower your body down, and at the same time move your right leg out to your side. Hold the squat while keeping your spine straight and abdominals pulled in. Exhale as you slowly stand back up and bring your right leg back to starting position. Repeat this on your left side and continue alternating legs while squatting. The weights can also be positioned at your sides instead of up by your shoulders. Repeat this for 1–3 sets of 12–16 repetitions on each side.

TRADITIONAL: LUNGE

Stand with your right foot forward and your left foot behind you about three feet. Hold weights in each hand at your sides. Keep your spine tall and your belly pulled in. Inhale and lower your body straight down toward

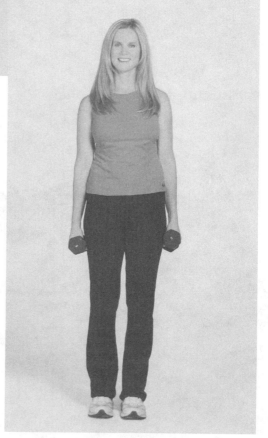

Moving Weighted Squat

Lunge on the Ball

the floor. Keep your front knee behind your toes. Exhale as you push up through your front heel and back to the starting position. Repeat this on each leg for 1–3 sets of 12–16 repetitions.

PROGRESSION: LUNGE ON THE BALL

Place one foot on top of a ball positioned behind you. Hold weights in each hand at your sides. Inhale and bend your knees and lower into a lunge position, keeping your spine tall and your abdominals contracted. Be sure to keep your knee behind your toes. Exhale and push through your front heel and slowly lift up to the starting position. Repeat this on each leg for 1–3 sets of 12–16 repetitions. This exercise is very advanced; if you do not feel comfortable with it, hold on to the wall for balance.

Turn Your Home into a Workout Center

When I saw Susie standing at my door, I had no idea that she would be bringing my soul's transformation with her. Her kind and obedient act not only changed my soul, it also changed the way I lived, the way I interacted . . . it even changed the way I viewed my home itself. I prayed over my house, making it a sanctuary for my spirit.

Not only is my home a sanctuary for me, it has also become a place for me to transform my body. The same can be true for you. You can transform your body from head to toe without even leaving your

● ● ●

"You can transform your body from head to toe without even leaving your home."

● ● ●

home. I know that for some people it can be a major ordeal just to get out of the house when the kids are small and not yet in school. I have a solution for you. Strengthen your body and keep your heart healthy by turning your home into a workout center. Here's the blueprint:

Kitchen Area

Equipment: soup cans or laundry detergent, chair

OVERHEAD PRESS (CHEST AND SHOULDERS)

Begin by standing or sitting up straight with your feet hip-width apart and abdominals engaged. Keep your shoulders down and chest up. Hold your soup cans at shoulder height with your palms facing forward. Exhale as you slowly lift both cans overhead. Inhale as you bring the cans down to the starting position. Repeat this exercise 12–15 times for 2–3 sets.

LATERAL RAISE (SHOULDERS)

Stand or sit up tall with feet shoulder-width apart with your abdominals contracted. Hold your soup cans or laundry detergent at your sides with your palms facing inward. Exhale as you lift the cans slowly from your sides until you reach shoulder height. Inhale and slowly lower the cans back down to your sides. Repeat this exercise 12–15 times for 2–3 sets.

KITCHEN CHAIR DIP
(TRICEPS)

Sit up tall in your kitchen chair and keep your abdominals contracted. Place your hands on your chair (almost under your bottom), thumbs in and fingers facing forward. Slide your bottom forward, just far enough that you clear the edge of the chair. Inhale and lower yourself down while keeping your back straight and belly pulled in. Exhale as you lift up, using only your arms (triceps). Repeat this 8–12 times for 2–3 sets.

KITCHEN WALL SIT
(LEGS AND LOWER BODY)

Start with your back against a wall and your feet about two feet away from the wall. Keep your back straight and your abdominals engaged. Inhale as you slide down the wall until your knees are at a ninety-degree angle. Hold this position for ten seconds and deep breathe! Exhale as you slide back up the wall to your starting position. Repeat this exercise 8-12 times.

BICEPS CURL
(BICEPS)

Sit or stand up tall with shoulders down and abdominals contracted. Hold your soup cans or laundry detergent with palms facing out, and your elbows next to the body. Exhale as you bend the elbows and lift the cans toward your shoulders without moving your elbows. Inhale and lower the cans to the starting position. Repeat this curl for 12–15 repetitions and 2–3 sets.

Family Room Area

Equipment: furniture and floor

SQUAT (QUADS, HIPS, THIGHS AND HAMSTRINGS)

Face away from a chair or a couch and stand up tall with feet hip-width apart and your abdominals contracted. Inhale and keep your knees behind your toes as you sit down on the couch for a few seconds. Exhale and contract the glutes (your bottom) and hamstrings (upper back leg muscles) as you lift off the couch into a tall standing position. Repeat this exercise again, but this time do not actually sit down on the couch, hover above it. Repeat for 12–15 repetitions and 1–3 sets.

STANDING LUNGE (MULTIPLE LOWER BODY MUSCLES)

Begin by standing in a split stance, holding onto your chair or couch if needed for balance. Remember to keep your back straight and your abdominals pulled in. Inhale and lower down toward the floor, keeping both knees at a ninety-degree angle. Do not allow your front knee to extend over your toe. Exhale as you push through your back heel and contract your glutes and push up without locking your knees. Repeat this exercise on this leg for 8–12 repetitions and then switch legs. Repeat both legs for 2–3 sets.

ABDOMINAL CRUNCH
(ABDOMINALS)

Lie down on the floor and place your lower legs on your couch with your knees bent at a ninety-degree angle. Place your hands across your chest or beside your head. Make sure you do not pull on your head during this exercise. Pull your belly button toward your spine. Exhale as you slowly contract your abdominals, bringing your shoulders about one or two inches off the floor and look toward your belly. Inhale and slowly lower back down to the floor. Repeat this exercise for 15–20 repetitions and 2–3 sets.

Shaped by God

After Susie asked about my healing, there was something inside of me that yearned to learn more about Jesus Christ and what He had to say. Heading home after picking up Candice at preschool, I was excited just knowing that I would get to spend time in His Word. With only a King James Version of the Bible, I thought it might be a little difficult for me to understand, but I decided to sit down at the kitchen table and give it a try.

At the table, I closed my eyes and asked God to help me understand what I was about to read. I knew I would need divine help comprehending what God had to say in His Word. My new friend Susie suggested I start by reading the New Testament so that I would learn about how Jesus lived while on the earth.

My first day in the Word, I read for hours in between caring for my daughters and waiting for my husband to come home for dinner. I had a voracious spiritual appetite and there didn't seem to be enough time in the day to feed my hunger for His Word. God was changing my heart, and I started to notice a total transformation taking place inside me.

In Galatians 2:19–20, Paul speaks about the transformation that happens when we turn our lives over to Christ: "For through the law I died to the law so that I might live for God. I have been crucified with Christ and I no longer live, but Christ lives in me. The life I live in the body, I live by faith in the Son of God, who loved me and gave himself for me" (NIV). My worldview changed once I experienced His truth for the first time.

• • •

"When we allow God to transform the way we think, we begin to blossom into a new person. We stop making excuses and start acting in faith."

• • •

When we allow God to transform the way we think, we begin to blossom into a new person. By studying His Word, we become motivated to make the necessary changes required to experience a life of peace. We stop making excuses and start acting in faith. And allowing God to work His will in our lives helps us when we face different storms that blow our way. With a Christ-centered mind-set, we can handle difficulties, knowing that He is in control.

Shaped by Prayer

RENEW MY MIND, HEART, BODY AND SPIRIT,
LORD JESUS. CHANGE ANYTHING ABOUT ME
THAT DOES NOT BRING GLORY OR HONOR TO
YOU, O GOD. MOLD ME AND EMBRACE ME AS
I WALK EACH DAY WITH YOU AT MY SIDE. YOU
ARE THE REASON I AM ALIVE, AND I PRAISE
YOU! YOU LOVE ME SO MUCH THAT YOU MET
ME RIGHT WHERE I WAS AND ACCEPTED ME
INTO YOUR FAMILY WITH ALL OF MY FLAWS.
THANK YOU FOR GIVING ME NEW LIFE.
HELP ME TO SHARE MY TESTIMONY WITH
OTHERS SO THAT THEY WILL EXPERIENCE
THE POWERFUL TRANSFORMATION THAT ONLY
TAKES PLACE IN KNOWING YOU. HELP THOSE
WHO DO NOT KNOW YOU TO OPEN UP THEIR
HEARTS AND LIVES TO YOU. IN THE NAME OF
JESUS CHRIST I PRAY, AMEN.

Chapter Seven

Center

> WHAT IS MORE, I CONSIDER EVERYTHING A LOSS
> COMPARED TO THE SURPASSING GREATNESS OF
> KNOWING CHRIST JESUS MY LORD, FOR WHOSE
> SAKE I HAVE LOST ALL THINGS. I CONSIDER THEM
> RUBBISH, THAT I MAY GAIN CHRIST.
>
> PHILIPPIANS 3:8 (NIV)

As I sat waiting at a traffic light one afternoon, I noticed two adolescent boys attempting to cross the busy four-lane highway. They stood on the curb, in the ready-to-run position, waiting for any slim opening to cross to the median. Defying danger, they set off, narrowly dodged several cars, and reached their midpoint destination. I noticed one of the boys wipe his hand across his forehead, as if to say, "Whew! That was a close one." They both looked anxious—clearly, they had never attempted such a feat before, and although they probably wouldn't have admitted it, they were scared. I was pretty sure that was the case, because instead of attempting to cross the rest of the way, they just plopped down, sitting cross-legged in the median. I drove on, praying they'd make it safely across before nighttime.

Those boys' adventure became a surprising lesson for me. Life whizzes by us just like those speeding cars, and like those boys, we are often scared by it. I took comfort that I, too, can metaphorically plop down in the median—in the center of my busy road—which is Christ.

I feel incredibly blessed that I can experience safety and security with a Christ-centered life. When He is the focal point in my life, there is no need to be anxious about anything. His plan for my life and yours is always beneficial, comforting, and eternal.

Our bodies have a median of sorts, too: our physical core. The core allows us to move with power and strength, while simultaneously protecting our body from injury, disease, and weakness. A physically strong core, coupled with the strength and security of a Christ-centered life, provides the confidence necessary to overcome any obstacle that crosses your path.

Shaped by Life

Shortly into my second marriage, I became pregnant with twin boys. My marriage was in shambles, but my love for these growing children was overwhelming and my newfound faith in Christ gave me transcendent peace. As I prayed for the boys in my womb, I had the unshakable sense that God would use them for His purposes. For what exactly, I didn't know. But I was confident that these two boys would become the beauty from my ashes.

Thirty-seven weeks into the pregnancy, at a routine doctor's appointment, I was told to immediately go to the hospital. The doctor explained that I had toxemia and the babies could be in danger if I did not deliver them soon. It felt like my insides were swimming in fluid. My weight gain was over eighty pounds, and I was experiencing high blood pressure. My husband met me in the emergency room, and we were immediately taken to a room to prepare for the delivery of my sons. One of them was breech, so a C-section was necessary.

Theresa's Top Three for Centering

1 Delight in life and find reasons to laugh . . . it'll lighten your load and strengthen your soul.

2 Use your body's core to originate your movements, and you will become stronger and better balanced.

3 Make Christ the center of your life. When He is at your core, you can handle any hardship that comes your way.

My son Carter Jeffrey was delivered first, weighing in at six pounds, fourteen ounces. Hunter had to be repositioned from his breech position, and exactly one minute later, he was born. He weighed six pounds, fourteen ounces—exactly the same as his brother.

After the doctor sewed up my incision, I was taken back to my room. I began shivering and shaking uncontrollably. The nurse placed warm blankets on me, but they felt like ice. I kept explaining that I was cold and that I couldn't control my shaking. The nurse retrieved the doctor, who discovered that I was hemorrhaging and needed an emergency blood transfusion. My blood pressure had plummeted.

As I shook in bed, waiting for the transfusion, it took all I had to focus on saying just one word: "Jesus." I think I assumed I would be seeing Him soon. I knew that my life was at risk, but somehow I wasn't worried. I was a child of God, and in that hospital room, His presence was as palpable as the blanket that covered me. I knew that He had sent His angels to comfort me and strengthen my body.

After the transfusion, I woke up feeling weak, but I knew that everything would be fine. I thanked God for sparing my life once again.

Between the special needs of the babies and taking care of the girls, life was very busy. My husband had fallen into a routine of not showing up for dinner, and sometimes not coming home for days at a time.

One Monday morning, I kissed the girls good-bye as they headed toward the school bus. After they left, my husband walked through the door, finally home from the weekend. Typically, when he came home, he went straight to bed. But on that day, he approached me immediately, a timid look on his face.

He said, "Don't take it personally, but I don't want to be married anymore. I'll be out of the house today."

When my first marriage dissolved after three-and-a-half years, I was devastated—embarrassed by the divorce, horrified of what my father would think, and shaken by my inability to save the marriage. But not this time. I was heartbroken, to be sure, that my second marriage, also three-and-a-half years long, was over. I wanted to believe that I could find a marriage full of love and maturity. But I was centered on Christ, and I knew that as long as my life revolved around Him, I would be safe. The Word of God says that He will never leave us or forsake us, and I was trying with all of my heart to hold on to that promise.

I knew what I had to do. Without a word, I picked up my boys, one in each arm, and calmly walked out the door. I placed them in their car seats and turned the wheel in the direction of my girls. And I left.

Nearly two years passed. I moved back to Kentucky, near my father. I was burdened by mounting financial struggles and doing my best as a working single mother. Finally, word came that my divorce was complete. The court established a child support requirement for my ex-husband, but he never paid anything. I tried to contact him, but had no success.

I was on my own . . . but not alone. God was the core of my family—and He was strengthening us.

Shaped by Fitness

The word "core" carries immense depth. Metaphorically, it is our center—our purest identity. Spiritually, it is what gives us hope, what holds us together, what strengthens our lives. Many folks use the phrase "accept Jesus into my heart," but for me it makes more sense to "accept Jesus into my core" because it is at my core—my identity—that I need Him most. After all, it is from the center that everything comes forth. Physically, the core is the literal center of our body, the most crucial muscle structure we have. Any movement we make should originate with our core muscles.

Our core (foundational) muscles help support our spine and back, and they keep our bodies stable and balanced. Most people think of abdominal muscles when they hear the word "core." But our body's core actually consists of twenty-nine muscles that surround our trunk and pelvis and that make up our abs and back. These muscles make it possible for us to stand up, bend and move as we shift our body weight and transfer energy.

When we move from our core, everything else in the body works more efficiently. Engaging your core muscles provides a strong brace of support for the entire body, which prevents injury.

Following is a list of the muscles that make up our core, and a corresponding exercise to strengthen each area. The spine will act as a stabilizer during these exercises, but make sure to maintain as much control and balance as possible.

● ● ●

"Physically, the core is the literal center of our body, the most crucial muscle structure we have. Any movement we make should originate with our core muscles."

● ● ●

TRANSVERSE ABDOMINIS: *Our deepest abdominal muscles, located below the belly button, under the obliques. These muscles act as a large belt that wraps around your spine for protection and stability.*

SCISSOR

Lie down on your back. Lift one leg parallel with the floor, and lift your other leg toward the ceiling. Keep your spine extended and abdominal muscles contracted. Exhale as you lift your shoulders and head off the floor. Look toward your belly. Inhale and place both hands on the leg reaching toward the ceiling. Exhale and alternate the position of your legs, lowering one and raising the other. Inhale and switch legs again. Repeat this cycle 5–10 times.

RECTUS ABDOMINIS: *This long muscle extends along the front of the abdomen. It is often referred to as the "six pack" muscle that becomes visible when a person has low body fat.*

BALL CRUNCH

Begin by lying supine on a stability ball, gently pressing your lower back against the ball. Place your hands beside your head or cross your arms in front of your chest. Contract your abdominal muscles. Exhale and curl up as you lift your torso off the ball. Hold this position for a few seconds. Inhale and lower back down while stretching the torso longer. Repeat for 12–16 repetitions and 1–3 sets.

INTERNAL OBLIQUE: *These muscles lie under the external oblique, running in the opposite direction.*

OBLIQUE CRUNCH

Begin by lying on your back on the floor. Contract your abdominals and keep your spine lengthened. Cross your left foot over your right knee and place your hands beside your head. Exhale and lift your shoulder blades off the floor, curl your upper body up, and then rotate diagonally across your body toward your left knee. Try not to force your elbow across your body. Inhale and slowly lower your body back down to the floor. Repeat sixteen times on this side and then switch to the other side. Repeat this entire exercise for 1–3 sets.

EXTERNAL OBLIQUE: *These muscles are on the side and front of the abdomen and make up our waist.*

SIDE LYING OBLIQUE (ON THE BALL)

Place yourself in a side lying position on a stability ball by resting your bottom knee on the floor and extending your top leg out with your foot on the floor. Your hands can be placed beside your head or cross your arms in front of your chest. Contract your abdominals and lengthen your spine. Exhale and lift your upper body off the ball while pulling your rib cage toward your hip. Hold this position for three to five seconds and then inhale and lower body to your starting position. Repeat this for 12–16 repetitions and then switch sides. Repeat this on each side for 1–3 sets.

ERECTOR SPINAE: *This group of three muscles runs from your neck to your lower back.*

SPINE EXTENSION

Lie face down on the floor with your hands extended over your head and your legs stretching behind you. Make sure your abdominals are contracted and your spine is extended. Exhale and lift your upper and lower body off the floor while keeping your head and neck in alignment with your spine. Hold this position for three to five seconds. Inhale and lower back down to the floor or hover above the floor for a challenge. Repeat this for 12–16 repetitions.

DEVELOPING YOUR POWERHOUSE WITH PILATES

Having strong core muscles (or, as it's called in Pilates, a powerhouse) came in handy for me as a single parent raising four children, because it allowed me to move quickly and powerfully through my daily tasks. The physical strength that came from the center of my body helped me to be able to work four jobs, do my laundry, fix dinner, take care of my children, and generally be on the go all the time—while feeling a comfortable amount of energy throughout. That's what a strong powerhouse provides. No other muscle group in your body supports you as thoroughly as your core, and nothing else provides such an enduring sense of energy either.

When I first discovered Pilates, I fell in love with its focus on the core. Every movement in Pilates initiates from the core, creating center strength while building muscles in other areas. Besides the strength Pilates provides, it also is a beautiful, dancelike, low-impact workout. When I am doing Pilates exercises, I feel empowered and graceful at the same time. I believe the best way to develop a strong powerhouse is through Pilates.

So what exactly is Pilates? Pilates is a series of stretching and strengthening exercises developed in the twentieth century by Joseph Pilates. He called his method "Contrology," which refers to the way the method encourages the use of the mind to control the muscles. It is an exercise program that focuses on the core postural muscles that help keep the body balanced and are essential to providing support for the spine. In particular, Pilates exercises teach awareness of breath, alignment of the spine, and strengthening of the deep torso muscles, which are important to help alleviate and prevent back pain. Pilates requires concentration and focus, because the body is moved through precise ranges of motion. Pilates caters to everyone, from beginner to advanced, with modifications shown for each exercise. You can perform the exercises on a mat, using your own body weight, or with the aid of various props, such as a stability ball, a small weighted ball, stretch bands, the Pilates circle, or foam rollers.

• ● •

"Pilates is a beautiful, dancelike, low-impact workout that initiates from the core."

• ● •

A typical Pilates workout includes a number of exercises performed in repetitions of ten. Each exercise is performed with attention to proper breathing techniques and abdominal control. To gain the maximum benefit, you should do Pilates at least two times per week. You should notice a body transformation and postural improvements within ten to twenty sessions.

Besides a strengthened core, Pilates promotes whole-person wellness by providing:

- improved flexibility

- increased muscle strength, particularly of the abdominal muscles, lower back, hips and buttocks (powerhouse muscles or core)

- balanced muscular strength on both sides of the body

- enhanced muscular control of the back and limbs

- improved stabilization of the spine

- greater awareness of posture

- improved physical coordination and balance

- relaxation of your shoulders, neck and upper back

- safe rehabilitation of joint and spinal injuries

- prevention of musculoskeletal injuries

- eased lower back pain

- uplifted mind and spirit

On pages 136 and 137 are two of my favorite Pilates exercises that will help you build a strong core. It doesn't take a ton of repetitions to build your powerhouse; it takes concentration, breathing, purposeful movement, and a willingness to take it step-by-step.

1. Lie down on your back. Lift your feet off the floor and bend your knees toward your chest, keeping the lower half of your legs parallel to the floor.

2. Exhale and lift your upper body, contract your rib cage toward your pelvis, and raise your arms off the mat, keeping them parallel to the floor.

3. Inhale and bring your knees toward your chest with your hands gently touching your lower legs.

4. Exhale and extend both legs out and arms straight up and over your head and shoulders. Maintain a neutral spine and strong abdominals.

5. Inhale and move your arms from behind your head out to your sides and bring them toward your legs as you bring your knees in toward your chest. Repeat this 5–10 times.

1. Begin by lying on your back with your legs extended out and your arms reaching over your head. Engage your powerhouse muscles and keep your spine neutral.

2. Inhale deeply, and lift your shoulders and upper body off the floor one vertebra at a time as you exhale and extend up over your legs, keeping your legs and feet on the floor and your eyes gazing toward your powerhouse muscles.

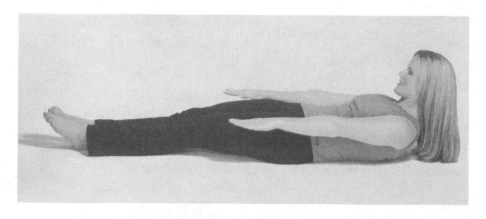

3. Inhale and roll back down to the floor one vertebra at a time while keeping your abdominals scooped in. Repeat this 5–10 times.

roll up / roll down

Laughing to the Core

My kids and I laugh together . . . a lot. Even when I was unmarried, low on resources, and lonely, we were all happy to be together. On weekends, the girls and I would watch old movies and *I Love Lucy* episodes, and the boys would add their own comic relief . . . they were always doing something silly or cute to get our attention. Laughter would fill our house and lighten up the seriousness of our situation.

Lucille Ball is my favorite comedienne of all time. She was beautiful, graceful, and always willing to sacrifice both for the sake of laughter. I love laughing with Lucy, but little did I know that she was practicing what researchers are now discovering about laughter: It's healthy for the soul *and* the body. Laughter is more than just medicine; it decreases stress hormones, and studies have shown that it decreases dopamine levels—which are normally associated with blood pressure. Studies have also shown that laughter activates our immune system. In a study published in the *Journal of Holistic Nursing*, patients were told one-liners after surgery and before pain medication was administered. Those exposed to humor perceived less pain when compared to patients who did not get a dose of humor as part of their therapy. And laughter also increases antibodies (immunoglobulin A), which fight upper respiratory tract infections.

● ● ●

"Laughing out loud burns calories. One hundred laughs burns the same amount of calories as approximately ten minutes of jogging."

● ● ●

For those of you trying to lose weight, I have more good news about laughter.

Laughing out loud burns calories. In fact, one hundred laughs (loosely defined, of course) burns the same amount of calories as approximately ten minutes of jogging. And, as if laughter didn't provide enough, laughter contracts—almost exclusively—your core muscles. The more you laugh, the more you develop your powerhouse and, in turn, increase your metabolism and energy levels.

Researchers say that the average four-year-old laughs approximately five hundred times per day. Conversely, the average adult is fortunate to laugh only four times a day. If we can work on increasing our ability to laugh, like children, that simple act would improve our health. The best part? Laughter is free of charge, readily available to anyone who wants to make a positive change toward whole-person wellness.

Shaped by God

After my second husband chose to leave me, my kids and I had very few material goods, but we had each other, and, above all, we had our faith in Christ. We learned how to live each day by depending on God to supply all of our needs. Looking back, I thank Him for allowing me to be sharpened and strengthened. It was difficult to be the only parent in the house, but with God at my center, I knew I had all I needed to raise my four children. Every morning, I poured my heart out to Him asking for help to make it through the day. When my house and car were taken from me because I could no longer afford to make the payments, God stepped in and provided us with an older model car and a tiny house. I learned to appreciate what God was willing to give us and not feel entitled to anything more. This season was more than a survival period; it poured concrete for my spiritual foundation—I felt broke, lonely, and hurt, but my core was whole.

Every night, I would read the Bible to my children before bedtime, and I watched as their faith increased eachday. When God's miracles happened in our family—and this was an everyday occurrence!—our faith was strengthened even more. My children saw firsthand the God that they had learned about in the Word. Because of my centeredness on God, my children were also centered on Him. They began depending on Him to help them with the smallest details, like their schoolwork, friendships, their hurts and disappointments. He became their spiritual Father and Savior.

The book of Romans says that our hope can only be found in Christ and we must rely on Him: "But hope that is seen is no hope at all. Who hopes for what he already has? But if we hope for what we do not yet have, we wait for it patiently" (NIV). When we wait on God and pray for Him to take care of us and our families, He moves mountains to answer our requests. Communing with our Father in heaven and reading His Word will help us to develop a spiritual core that is immovable when life's disasters try to destroy our peace.

• • •

"God promises to be our greatest powerhouse, supplying our every need, regardless of how challenging, painful, or impossible life may seem."

• • •

If you reflect back on your life, I can almost guarantee that you have seen your share of miracles along the way. When life spins out of control, we can activate our center and live each day with peace and His supernatural power, regardless of what is going on around us. Hebrews 11:1 says, "Faith is the confidence that what we hope for will actually happen; it gives us assurance about things we cannot see." Waiting on God to act is the hardest part, and I still have not mastered this skill. But I do know that when we wait on the Lord and continue to believe that He will work things out, a supernatural high happens.

God promises to be our greatest powerhouse, supplying our every need, regardless of how challenging, painful or impossible life may seem. Following are some faith-building Scriptures that will strengthen your soul. Read them out loud and believe them in your heart. Memorize them and rely on them every day. Just as abdomen workouts strengthen our physical core, so does memorization and meditation on God's Word strengthen our spiritual core.

* * *

AND MY GOD WILL MEET ALL YOUR NEEDS ACCORDING TO
HIS GLORIOUS RICHES IN CHRIST JESUS.
—PHILIPPIANS 4:19 (NIV)

* * *

FOR GOD HAS SAID, "I WILL NEVER FAIL YOU. I WILL NEVER
FORSAKE YOU." THAT IS WHY WE CAN SAY WITH CONFIDENCE,
"THE LORD IS MY HELPER, SO I WILL NOT BE AFRAID.
WHAT CAN MERE MORTALS DO TO ME?"
—HEBREWS 13:5—6

* * *

• • •

"I TELL YOU THE TRUTH, IF YOU HAVE FAITH AS SMALL AS A
MUSTARD SEED, YOU CAN SAY TO THIS MOUNTAIN, 'MOVE FROM HERE TO
THERE' AND IT WILL MOVE. NOTHING WILL BE IMPOSSIBLE FOR YOU."
—MATTHEW 17:20 (NIV)

• • •

"EVERYTHING IS POSSIBLE FOR HIM WHO BELIEVES."
—MARK 9:23 (NIV)

• • •

GOD, WHO HAS CALLED YOU INTO FELLOWSHIP WITH HIS SON
JESUS CHRIST OUR LORD, IS FAITHFUL.
—1 CORINTHIANS 1:9 (NIV)

• • •

Write these truths on your heart, knowing that you are centered on the one true God, who gives and takes away.

Shaped by Prayer

YOU, O GOD, ARE MY ROCK AND MY
REDEEMER! YOU ARE THE ALPHA AND THE
OMEGA, AND YOU REIGN ETERNALLY! I PRAY
THAT YOU WILL HELP ME TO STAY FOCUSED
AND CENTERED ON YOUR TRUTH AND WORD
DAILY. MAY MY LIFE BE PURPOSEFUL BECAUSE
YOU ARE MY STRONGHOLD. YOU DIRECT AND
GUIDE ME EACH DAY AS I DEPEND ON YOUR
UNFAILING LOVE. KEEP MY BODY HEALTHY
AND STRONG AS I KEEP MY EYES FIXED ON
YOU, MY GOD, MY REDEEMER.

AMEN.

Chapter Eight

Balance

There is beauty in balance. The graceful ballerina, rising and falling in rhythmic motion, gives evidence of it. The earth is her balance beam. She is stunning as she floats and glides from place to place, seemingly without effort.

What if you could be that ballerina, properly balanced, gliding through your daily activities? It *is* possible to be so graceful, steady and controlled. But maintaining healthy balance in our lives requires effort; we must become emotionally, physically, and spiritually stable. If one or several areas in our lives are out of balance, we become unstable, and, in many ways, we begin to tip over.

Achieving the right balance for my own life is still the most challenging task I face. I have learned that becoming balanced means setting priorities. God comes first, followed by a healthy lifestyle. And just as the ballerina was taught by a master instructor, we can choose to pattern our lives after true perfection, Christ.

Shaped by Life

In the fall of 1995, I was working at a dance studio as a children's dance instructor. At the end of every class, it was hard not to notice the only man in the studio waiting faithfully for his daughter Layla every week. His name was Robin, and he was also divorced. There was something about him that roused my interest, and after several conversations, I felt sure he was interested in me, too.

But a few months went by, and no matter how much I sensed he would, Robin did not approach me for a date. Fall came and went, Christmas passed, and still no date. We talked frequently after class and got along quite well, so I couldn't understand what was holding him back. Even though I had been divorced twice, I still hadn't sworn off marriage. Somehow, I knew that if I found the right man, I could find the stability and peace in a relationship that I had always longed for. I wasn't sure if Robin was that man, but I wanted the opportunity to find out.

In January, dance class resumed, and I again began to see Robin there with Layla. One afternoon, I had a strong urge from the Spirit to write Robin a note. I argued with myself, saying that I was just being impatient. After all, he had not approached me and I had never asked a man out before. But the urge got stronger, and again I told myself that he didn't deserve my attention if he hadn't asked for it. But after a while, I couldn't get the thought out of my head, so I reluctantly grabbed a yellow notepad and scribbled, "Maybe we could go out and talk sometime." After class, as the studio filled with parents, I hesitated and then called his name out loud. Robin turned to me, and I handed him the yellow note. He put it in his pocket and walked out the door, holding his daughter's hand.

A few weeks passed, and Robin stopped showing up at the dance studio. I couldn't imagine how he could not only ignore my note but ignore me altogether. What was his problem? Waiting for a man to call did not fit my agenda, so I decided to write him off.

One evening after class, I'd just had the thought that perhaps I wouldn't have to see him again—and I would be glad for it. Any man who ignored such a vulnerable step didn't deserve me. But, as many comedies go, that evening Robin returned to pick up Layla. I turned my back to him and busied myself with computer work. He walked over to my desk and said, "I have arranged for us to go out this Friday evening." Just like that.

I wanted to ignore him right back, but for some reason—and I think I know why—I told him that it would be fine.

When Friday arrived, I reflected on how the evening came about. My stubbornness and pride started to flare up, and I decided I was going to call the date off. My daughters were excited about my date, but I could tell them that I wasn't feeling well. I picked up the phone to call Robin and then realized that I didn't have his phone number—he had never given it to me. I sat down on my bed and prayed. "Your will be done God, not mine." I didn't feel like going out, but I knew I couldn't stand him up; he was probably on his way over to my house at that moment.

Later that night, I was so glad I hadn't been able to cancel the date. Our time together was what you picture when you imagine the perfect first date. We spoke about everything from our shared faith to our children—in addition to Layla, who was ten, he also had Adrian and Ethan, who were fourteen and sixteen, respectively. My Christina was fourteen, Candice was eleven, and Jeffrey and Hunter were four. He even told me why he had taken so long to ask me out: He thought I was out of his league and that I was putting out intimidating signals. I felt guilty, but mostly I felt thankful for how the Lord had led me to initiate our first date.

After our second date, we were discussing marriage. We knew that God had placed us together for His purposes. And on February 29, 1996, Robin proposed to me in my small living room while my daughters watched from their bedroom door. After he proposed, I realized that it was a leap year. With a knowing smile, he explained that there was a reason for his leap-year proposal.

"We are taking a leap of faith," he said, "and I know our faith will be honored."

He was right. We got married less than a month later, on March 24, and our marriage is full of God's blessings and built on His foundation.

Before I married Robin, my whole life had felt like a spinning top. I was never stable, never balanced. I had been an adopted child, living in fear of my family. I'd had two unhealthy marriages and four children to care for on my own. I had little clue who I was or where I fit. Christ had become my core, and I had been praying that the Lord would bring more balance to my life, which He did. God gave me Robin, who helped give emotional, financial, and physical stability to our family. I believe that the Father can bring us balance in many ways: through His Spirit, through the support of friends and family, through a church home, and other avenues as well. But the Lord knew that I needed Robin, and I thank Him every day for that gift.

Theresa's Top Three for Balance

1 Be honest with yourself and God about everything in your life that throws you off balance, and then trust that He will provide the stability you need.

2 Challenge your body to become more balanced by exercising with a stability ball and other counterbalance techniques.

3 Pattern your life after Christ, and your leaps of faith will land steady and sure.

Shaped by Fitness

During one of my heart-related hospital stints, my poor sweet husband stayed in the room to keep me company during the night. I had fallen asleep, and after he finished watching the football game, he was quietly preparing the chair to be his bed. He had leaned over to retrieve his blanket, using the back of the chair as support, when the chair footrest collapsed, sending his weight over the chair and onto his hand. His broken hand required surgery, and his story illustrates the innately human need to be balanced.

But balance is more than keeping your weight evenly distributed; it is the process of pursuing spiritual, physical, and mindful harmony. Balance is life's equilibrium. For example, each of a car's four tires work in harmony to bring about a smooth and gentle ride. If one tire falls off, the car loses control and will likely crash.

Maintaining control and balance is best achieved with the use of counterbalances. The Bible tells us that when we are at our weakest, God is at His best. He is strong enough to counterbalance our difficulties with supernatural power, which brings us back to stability. Fixing our minds on things that are noble and true, protecting and maintaining our bodies, and placing God first in our lives can bring us peace and harmony.

Counterbalances exist in fitness too. They are the exercises you do in unstable environments that force your body to adjust to the in-

> **"**Maintaining control and balance is best achieved with the use of counterbalances. The Bible tells us that when we are at our weakest, God is at His best.**"**

stability and thus become acutely balanced. A small but perfect example of counterbalances is standing on one leg. When we balance on one leg, we change the natural position of our bodies and immediately activate our sense of balance. Another perfect counterbalance is the stability ball, which puts us on a nongeometric foundation, causing us to correct for the instability.

The Stability Ball

I began working out with the stability ball the same year that Robin and I were married. The sense of balance that Robin had brought to my life was palpable and resounding, so when I learned about the stability ball from a friend at the studio, I knew it was something I was interested in. Balance was a new reality for me, and I wanted—as I always do with life's lessons—to implement it into my workouts.

Since then, I have used the stability ball more than any other tool in my classes. All of my students will bear witness to this—I am borderline obsessed with the stability ball! I even use the ball at home, while working on my computer. In fact, I wrote this entire book sitting on my stability ball. I can tell you first hand that typing for hours while sitting on the ball made my back feel aligned and my abdominals strong.

So what is the stability ball? The stability ball is like a large, sturdy beach ball. It

> "I use the stability ball while working on my computer. Typing for hours while sitting on the ball makes my back feel aligned and my abdominals strong."

challenges our workouts by placing our bodies in an unstable environment, which forces us to re-create balance without having two feet on solid ground. The ball improves balance and flexibility, and strengthens the core, spine, hip flexors, and leg muscles. I highly encourage you to buy a stability ball for yourself or use one at your gym.

When purchasing a stability ball, there are a few things to consider. I recommend buying an antiburst ball, which won't pop easily and can hold up to five hundred pounds. I avoid using the shiny looking balls, which are challenging to work with because of their slick surface. I use a ball with a thicker and stickier outer surface. Fitness balls come in different sizes, and choosing the correct size depends on your height. To determine correct size, you should be able to sit on a ball with your knees bent at a ninety-degree angle. If you are purchasing a ball, find a good size for you using this list:

- Up to 5'4" use a 45 cm

- 5'5" to 5'7" use 55 cm

- 5'8" to 6' use 65 cm

- Over 6' use 75 cm

Now, for the fun part. Here are my three favorite ball exercises.

Triceps Ball Dip

TRICEPS BALL DIP

My favorite strength exercise on the ball is the triceps dip. Most people have difficulty with this exercise at first because of the balance challenge. Plus, the dip off the ball is an advanced exercise that really challenges our triceps muscles. If you want to define and tone up your triceps quickly, this is the exercise you should be doing at least three times a week. Your triceps may be a little sore after you have completed three sets of 12–15 repetitions!

Sit on the ball with your hands under your bottom and your fingers pointing forward. Sit up tall and make sure your abdominals are engaged. Inhale as you lift your bottom off the ball and place it close to the ball. Both knees should be bent at ninety degrees and feet placed hip width apart. Lower your bottom toward the floor and maintain a straight spine. Exhale as you lift up, pressing into the ball while keeping your shoulders down. Remember, your triceps should be doing the work. Repeat this exercise for 12–15 repetitions and then rest for thirty seconds. You can repeat the dips for two more sets.

To make this exercise easier, place the ball against the wall for more balance. Do one set of 8–12 repetitions and then rest for one minute. Repeat this exercise for another set of 8–12 repetitions.

BALL OBLIQUE CURL

Lie faceup on the ball with your lower back resting on it. Cross your arms in front of your chest or position your hands at the sides of your head. Pull in your abdominals and lengthen your spine. Exhale and curl up and rotate to the left side. Inhale and lower your back down, stretching your spine and abdominals. Repeat this on the other side and continue alternating sides for 16 repetitions on both sides. Repeat for 1–3 sets.

Ball Oblique Curl

BALL KNEE TUCK

Drape yourself over the ball and walk out on your hands until your shins are resting on the top of the ball (push-up position). Inhale and bend your knees and bring the ball in toward your chest, keeping the abdominals contracted. Exhale and push your legs back behind you. Repeat this for 1–3 sets of ten repetitions.

Ball Knee Tuck

Supine Ball Pass

SUPINE BALL PASS

Start by lying on your back (supine) holding the ball straight up over your head with your legs extended straight up. Make sure you are contracting your abdominals and your spine stays neutral. Exhale and put the ball between your feet, squeezing the ball in place, and lower both arms overhead and legs toward the floor. Inhale and bring your arms back up as you take the ball in your hands, lowering your arms overhead with the ball and your legs toward the floor. Keep your back straight and abdominals contracted. Repeat this for 1–3 sets of 12–16 repetitions.

Step Aerobics for Improved Balance and Strength

Step aerobics has been part of my life since the late 1980s. It's a foolproof way to increase your balance. The step is a raised platform, typically four inches high, on which you step up and down. Depending on your fitness level, the steps can be increased up to twelve inches by adding risers under each side of the step. Most step videos and classes use music that accompanies the step routine.

Not only does the step strengthen your heart, lungs and lower body, it also works your abdominal muscles. Raising and lowering yourself on the step requires your abdominal muscles to stabilize so that you can keep stepping without falling. By engaging your core muscles while stepping, you keep your body balanced.

Most people who are not familiar with step aerobics shy away from it because they fear there is too much pressure placed on their knees and joints. But, in fact, step places minimal pressure on the joints, knees, and legs; it just works the muscles around the knees, which is where that sense of discomfort comes from. In terms of safety, doing step is actually comparable to walking.

When doing step, there are specific posture details to keep in mind:

- Keep your neck relaxed and straight.

- Always keep your knees soft and not locked.

- Stand up tall (back straight) and contract your abdominals.

- Your shoulders should stay down, away from your ears.

- As you step onto the platform, stand up tall and do not bend from the hips.

- Place your entire foot on the platform, with your heel landing first.

- Make sure your heels are not hanging over the edge.

- Step quietly by using the muscles in your legs. Pounding could cause an injury.

- Keep an eye on the platform, but try not to look down too often.

- Exhale as you step up on the platform and inhale as you step back down to the floor.

Here are a few step exercises that you can try at home or at the gym. If you don't have a professional-grade step, no problem. Just use a bottom stair or find a sturdy platform. After you have mastered the basic steps, use the advanced exercises.

BASIC STEP

Begin by leading with your right foot as you step up on the platform followed by your left foot. (Step up right, step up left.) Step down with your right foot and then your left foot.

If you feel ready, add your arms by reaching them overhead when you step up and lowering them as you step down. Repeat this for four sets of sixteen repetitions. (Stepping up and down will count as one repetition.) Repeat this by leading with your left foot.

ADVANCED: BICEPS CURL WITH STEPPING

Hold a dumbbell in each hand at your sides with your elbows in close to your body. Step up and lift the weights up (biceps curl), and lower the weights to your sides when you step down on the floor.

V-STEP

Lead with your right foot as you step up wide; then your left foot steps up wide. Your right foot steps down on the floor near the middle of the step and then your left foot steps down. Your hands can be placed on your hips or on your legs.

Repeat this step for two sets of sixteen repetitions. Repeat by leading with your left foot.

ADVANCED: FRONT RAISE WITH STEPPING

Holding a dumbbell in each hand at your sides, step up wide and raise the weights up to shoulder height; then lower the weights as you step back down to the floor.

KNEE LIFT

Step up with your right foot and lift your left knee. Arms can reach overhead on the way up and lower down as you step back down to the floor. Repeat sixteen knee lifts and then lead with your left foot and raise your right knee for sixteen repetitions.

ADVANCED: SHOULDER PRESS WITH STEPPING

Holding a dumbbell in each hand, lift them up to your shoulders. As you step up, lift the weights overhead when you lift your knee and then lower them to shoulder level as you step back down.

Shaped by God

I am still amazed at how God has worked in my family's life. For instance, my kids and I had prayed for years that God would send a man who loved Him first and who would love each of us as his own. When Robin came into my life, I knew there was something special about him and that kept my attention. But my idea of how Robin should pursue me was not God's idea at all. However, when I released my situation to God, He began unfolding His plan.

The Scripture says, "Don't worry about anything; instead, pray about everything. Tell God what you need, and thank him for all he has done. If you do this, you will experience God's peace, which is far more wonderful than the human mind can understand. His peace will guard your hearts and minds as you live in Christ Jesus" (Philippians 4: 6–7). Good things are worth waiting for and are best when relinquished to Christ. Anything else creates a spiritual and emotional imbalance. When we choose to take our own path and not God's—when we decide that our path will take us farther—we sacrifice the ultimate stability, which is God's pleasure.

"When we choose to take our own path and not God's—when we decide that our path will take us farther—we sacrifice the ultimate stability, which is God's pleasure."

Dig down deep in your heart and be honest with yourself and God about everything in your life that throws you off balance. Take those concerns to Him, and then trust that He will provide the very best for you. Miraculous things will start to happen if you watch and listen to how God can orchestrate balance in your life. He is the master dance instructor after all, training you to walk through life with the beauty and balance of a ballerina. With Christ, you will have the supernatural balance of someone walking in grace.

Shaped by Prayer

YOU ANSWERED MY PRAYERS, LORD, AND HEARD MY CRY. HOW CAN I REPAY YOUR KINDNESS AND MERCY? I WILL LIVE EACH DAY AS A GIFT FROM YOU. THANK YOU FOR BRINGING BALANCE INTO MY LIFE. I PRAY THAT WHEN I BECOME UNBALANCED, YOU WILL COME ALONGSIDE ME AND PLACE ME BACK WHERE I NEED TO BE. HELP ME TO STAY ON YOUR ROAD OF RIGHTEOUSNESS AS YOU BALANCE MY LIFE WITHIN YOU. MY DAYS ARE YOURS, AND I ASK THAT YOU WILL ARRANGE MY PLANS AND SCHEDULES ACCORDING TO YOUR WILL FOR MY LIFE. IN THE NAME OF JESUS I PRAY, AMEN.

Chapter Nine

Endure

> MY CHILD, LISTEN TO ME AND DO AS I SAY, AND
> YOU WILL HAVE A LONG, GOOD LIFE. I WILL TEACH
> YOU WISDOM'S WAYS AND LEAD YOU IN STRAIGHT
> PATHS. IF YOU LIVE A LIFE GUIDED BY WISDOM, YOU
> WON'T LIMP OR STUMBLE AS YOU RUN. CARRY OUT MY
> INSTRUCTIONS; DON'T FORSAKE THEM. GUARD THEM,
> FOR THEY WILL LEAD YOU TO A FULFILLED LIFE.
>
> PROVERBS 4:10—13

Willpower is wonderful and strength can be significant, but I have found that endurance is one of the most desirable characteristics. Endurance is the ability to continue when you'd much rather quit. All the willpower and strength in the world cannot carry a person through the most trying of times or the most physically exhausting experiences. Only endurance gives us the ability to *keep on*.

Still, I cannot stress enough the importance of keeping our bodies physically fit and our spirits tuned to God's strength so that we can endure trials and hardships. Whether it is surviving the summer heat, beating the odds of cancer, or meeting whatever other challenges come our way, we must be prepared to endure. I know from personal experience that this is true. Because I trained my heart and lungs through cardiovascular exercise, I was able to endure a very tough personal struggle.

Shaped by Life

August in Kentucky is a meteorological beast. This two-headed monster pounds us with the "Double H boys": high heat and high humidity. Ironically, August, my birth month, is also the month in which I have encountered a surprising amount of pivotal personal changes. Yet for some odd reason, the seasonal challenges that happen in August often motivate me to go into strict training.

Early one August morning in 2007, my running partner Jackie and I set off to pace away our routine four-mile run.

Even for Kentucky, it seemed exceptionally humid that morning. I have always been one to perspire relatively easily, but on that day, sweat was pouring down my face and soaking through my shirt before we even reached our first mile. We both commented on the early morning heat and then continued our conversation.

Something seemed different about this particular morning, though. By the time our run was in full swing, I felt overwhelming dizziness and nausea. I blamed it on the heat, so Jackie and I decided to walk for a few minutes.

Little did I know that I was about to experience a recurrence of my greatest physical challenge and one of the hardest tests of my endurance.

After teaching my fitness class that morning, I made an appointment with a cardiologist, something I was terrified of doing because of my horrific experience with doctors in the past. But that morning, the combined awareness of my health history and my current physical struggle suggested that something wasn't right, and I had no other choice but to turn to the doctors.

It had been several years since my last heart checkup, when the doctor had said that my heart was fine. I looked like the picture of health, he said. He told me not to return unless I was experiencing a problem. "You are an athlete. There's nothing to worry about," he had said. But everything felt so familiar . . .

On the morning of the run, I recalled the words of my doctor. Although I may have been "the picture of health," I decided the way I felt warranted a second opinion.

After a few tests, my new doctor recommended that I see a surgeon. The cardiologist's diagnosis: The previously repaired hole had reopened and needed to be closed. I was stunned. How could a person in such good cardiovascular health encounter not one, but two instances of heart defect?

Nonetheless, a few weeks later, Robin and I found ourselves preparing for my surgery. All the tests had shown that not only did I have a large gaping hole in my heart, but I also had some veins that were in the wrong place, along with a stretched-out tricuspid valve. My doctor encouraged me by saying, "While this is a risky procedure, I know your heart can handle it because you are so cardiovascularly strong."

I felt a peace about the surgery. Although I was shocked that the hole had returned in full force—and that it had happened during the height of my physical fitness—I was thankful that, if nothing else, my physical strength would be one of the greatest resources for my recovery. I knew my heart could endure much, not only because I had trained it so thoroughly, but most importantly because Christ was my strength.

The alarm clock rang at 4:15 AM, and I knew it was going to be a long day. As I walked into the bathroom to wash my face, I physically felt God's presence all around me. I was standing on holy ground in that bathroom, basking in His awesomeness. God's presence was embracing my soul, offering divine peace and comfort. I slipped on the shirt Candice had made especially for my surgery, which had a heart on it and a Scripture from Isaiah. I looked in the mirror and said, "It's time, Lord. Let's go."

My children came to my room, gave me big hugs, and said they would see me soon, right after my surgery. I smiled at each of them and looked into their eyes so that they could see the strength of Christ within me. I wanted them to know that I was not afraid and that with Christ at my side, everything would turn out the way it was meant to. I wanted them to draw their inner strength from the same source that gave me direction and had given me new life. I left for the hospital with Robin that morning saying, "I will not die, but live to proclaim the works of the Lord." I accepted the fact that I had to go through this trial in order for His greater plan to take place in my life. I looked forward to the days that would follow my surgery.

I was in the operating room for seven hours. The surgeon finally met with Robin and Christina. They told me later that they knew everything was all right just by looking at the doctor's face. Smiling broadly, she explained the procedure. "Theresa's physical strength allowed us to complete everything we wanted to do. We patched the hole, rerouted the vein that was going into the wrong side of the heart, and repaired and tightened the tricuspid valve. In a little while we will be moving her to CCU and you will be able to see her. I knew she could do it."

And Robin told me that in that moment, the doctor's smile was contagious.

Shaped by Fitness

Cardiovascular exercise is the foundational building block of physical endurance. Developing endurance is a process; it takes time, energy and dedication. You must be determined to live a life that is healthy and full of energy. No one can make you take that first step to exercise, but just think: There are few things more motivating than hearing someone else's success story, right? Then imagine what it would feel like to share yours. Allow the reciprocal effect to kick-start your fitness routine. When a student takes my class for the first time, I am motivated to work harder. And I am reminded of my own first experience.

Cardiovascular exercise has saved my life. Without a strong cardiovascular foundation, I would not be here today explaining the virtues of exercise. So what is it about cardio that makes our bodies so fit? Technically speaking, cardiovascular exercise is any activity that uses large muscle groups in a rhythmical, continuous motion and increases muscular stamina. In other words, cardio is what trains our hearts to withstand intense activity—it gives us endurance.

The best part about cardio is that you can do it anywhere: in a gym, outside, even at home. Whether you choose to take a brisk walk, swim, cycle, go hiking, dance in your home, jump rope, jog stairs, play sports, run, or attend a group fitness class, cardio is one of the most available sources of exercise there is.

Building endurance with cardio takes time and ideally it involves careful attention to your heart rate. As you develop more and more cardiovascular endurance, make sure that you are working at an intensity level that will strengthen your heart and lungs—no more, no less. The best way to test your heart rate is with a monitor, but you can also measure it manually.

A heart monitor lets you know if you are working too hard for your body to handle or if you need to increase your intensity level. Do you ever wonder how many calories you burn in an exercise class? A monitor calculates the number of calories you burn in an exercise session. There are some trainers who have you count your heart rate by placing your fingers

● ● ●

"Cardiovascular exercise has saved my life. Without a strong cardiovascular foundation, I would not be here today explaining the virtues of exercise."

● ● ●

on your pulse and counting how many beats per minute. But that is an inaccurate way to determine your heart rate, and most health professionals steer clear. For that reason, in order to get an accurate number, it's best to get a heart monitor. This is especially important if you have a history of heart disease, high blood pressure or other high-risk health complications.

If you don't have access to a monitor, you

can test your heart rate with the "talk test." Simply put, if you can talk during exercise but still feel a little breathless at the same time, you're about right.

A lot of fitness and health facilities use the "rate of perceived exertion" chart for manual heart rate monitoring. This chart is a scale of numbers from six to twenty, and the numbers represent how your body feels during exercise. Number six represents no exertion and twenty means maximum exertion. It's important to note that sweating is not a good indicator of your intensity level during exercise. Some people sweat a lot easier than others, so use one of the other tests in order to assess your heart rate and adjust your intensity level as needed.

Theresa's Top Three for Endurance

1 Incorporate a thirty-minute walk—or your favorite exercise—into each day, and use that time to talk to God.

2 Bring water wherever you go, whether driving the car, working, shopping or traveling, and especially while exercising.

3 Embrace the stresses in your life and thank God that you will come through them a stronger person, better able to endure what comes your way.

Here is a simple formula for determining what your maximum heart rate should be: 220 minus your age. Whatever number you get, you should not exceed it when exercising. A proper aerobic training zone—or your "target heart rate"—falls between fifty-five percent and eighty-five percent of your maximum heart rate.

Whatever direction you take toward cardiovascular fitness, select an activity that is compatible with your personality. Some people prefer working on machines like the elliptical, treadmill, spinning bike or stair climber, while others prefer taking their workout outside and walking, power walking, running, cycling, participating in team sports or swimming. If I had to suggest one of the best forms of cardiovascular activity walking would be at the top of the list.

Remember that endurance takes time to build, so no matter what activity you choose (although I do recommend varying activities), do it three to five times a week for twenty to thirty minutes. As you gain endurance, and you will, increase the intensity, frequency and length of the exercise.

Here are a few more creative ideas that you may want to request from your group instructor, or just try at home or in a park with some friends.

As I said before, the stability ball is one of my favorite pieces of equipment. The ball is so versatile and can be used to increase physical endurance by simply bouncing up and down while increasing the heart rate. The best part is that the ball seems to release the inner child within us. I use it in almost every class I teach, and I encourage my students to purchase the ball and to use it at home to increase their core strength and

Bounce Squat

endurance. If using the ball at home, try seated jumping jacks and bounce squats.

The bounce squat is another of my favorite cardio/strength exercises. Begin by sitting up tall on the ball with your feet hip-width apart and your hands on either side of your hips. Contract your abdominal muscles. Exhale and push off the ball into a half squat, while keeping your fingertips on the ball. Inhale and sit back down. I like to rev up the exercise this way: As you exhale and push off the ball, stand up tall and raise your arms over your head. Inhale and sit back down on the ball. Repeat this for 1–3 sets of sixteen repetitions.

Step classes are a wonderful way to tone the lower body and get a fantastic cardiovascular workout. If you don't have access to a gym, use a chair, stool, or actual stairs. Start by stepping up onto whatever object works for you, alternating feet in a steady motion. After you get comfortable with that movement, try adding kicks by pulling your knee to your chest as you rise mid-step. After a while, you may be able to add little hops to your steps—hops increase the intensity of the workout threefold, which of course increases your endurance in turn. Play some energetic music while you step—it will not only add rhythm to your movements, it'll also make the exercise more enjoyable.

Cardio Soul

For achieving improved strength and greater endurance, my comprehensive cardio soul workout is a winner. It is one of the best choices for exercise since it combines cardio, strength training, and core strengthening, all in the same workout. Do each step continuously, not stopping for breaks. It's important to keep your heart rate up during the entire exercise.

This workout can be done anywhere you choose: at home, outside, in the gym, at work, on vacation. The plan is far from boring and will keep you motivated and energized. Keep in mind that it is rewarding to work out with a partner, and this is the perfect exercise to do together.

You will need a jump rope, a child's small ball, and both a light and a heavier set of dumbbells (something like two and five pounds, respectively). Before starting the actual workout, prepare your body for exercise with a simple warm-up. For five to eight minutes, walk or jog, focusing on moving all of the big muscles in the body. If you choose to do this exercise in your home, march in place or walk back and forth on your driveway.

Once the warm-up is over, it's time to jump rope for three minutes. Jumping rope is not for everyone, especially if you are just starting out. So, another exercise you could do instead of jumping rope is alternating knee lifts while reaching your arms overhead or marching in place. Just keep moving at a more intense pace than the warm-up for three continuous minutes.

Next, grab your heavier set of dumbbells and hold them at your sides as you begin to do walking lunges. Step forward with your right leg and lower your upper body down, while keeping the back upright and maintaining balance. Inhale as you go down and make sure your toes are in front of your knee. Using mainly your back leg, push up to a standing position as you exhale and then bring your left leg forward and lunge. Continue doing the walking lunges for two minutes.

Walking Lunge

Vertical Leg Crunch

Core work is next with two minutes of vertical leg crunches on the floor while holding the child's play ball in between your feet. Keep your legs straight up as you curl toward your belly button. Remember to exhale on the curl up and inhale on the way down.

Grab your lighter weights and place them above your shoulders as you prepare to squat. Your feet should be shoulder width apart. Inhale as you squat, keeping the spine lengthened, and exhale as you stand back up and lift the weights overhead. During the squat, wiggle your toes and make sure there is no extra pressure on them or your knees. Continue the squat and shoulder press for two minutes.

Squat with Weights

Pick up the heavier weights again and hold them at your sides. Move the squat as you step out to your left side and then back to the middle and then step squat to your right side. Inhale as you squat down and exhale as you stand back up. Move the squat from side to side for one minute.

Lie down for core work and get ready to do two minutes of reverse curls. Lift your feet off the floor, bend your knees ninety degrees, contract your abdominals into your spine and roll your hips toward you. Keep your arms at your sides, exhale as you lift and inhale as you lower.

Now, go back to the beginning and repeat this workout two more times. Then cool down with a five-minute walk and then a dynamic stretch.

Continue doing this workout plan and change it as you progress. Your endurance will increase at a surprising pace if you do this workout three to five days a week!

Nutrition and Endurance: Water, Water, Water

My first experience with teaching aerobics and giving tips on wellness and nutrition was instructing a small group of ladies at my apartment complex in Omaha, Nebraska. Just a few weeks into our workout, the ladies began asking me questions about diet and nutrition. I felt responsible for our group and decided to find out all I could about the combination of a proper diet and exercise. I gave the ladies some basic dos and don'ts.

But the most important piece of advice I gave these ladies—and that I continue to give all my students, as it relates to building their endurance levels—was to *drink water*.

Most people believe that they drink plenty of water, but most of those same people are mistaken. According to the Food and Nutrition Board, it is recommended that women consume ninety-one ounces and men consume 125 ounces, respectively per day. Eighty percent of our hydration should come from drinking water, and the other twenty percent from food. Ask yourself: Are you providing your body with proper hydration? If not, it's time to start. Drinking plenty of water helps remove toxins from the body and transports nutrients to the cells. Water is the most important nutrient for sustaining life.

Drink water when you are thirsty instead of reaching for a diet or sugary drink or your favorite flavored coffee. On the road to endurance, hydration is key, yet sodas and excess coffees actually dehydrate you. They are counterproductive. Years ago, I used to drink diet drinks frequently. Instead of becoming healthier, I started to gain weight and experienced a lot of headaches. I'm not the only one, either. Tests have shown that diet drinks and sugary beverages alike make us gain weight and are dangerous for our health.

When you add exercise to your daily routine, your water consumption needs to increase even more. I often remind my students to bring bottled water with them to the gym and take sips of it during the workout. It is easy to become dehydrated and not even know it.

Since twenty percent of our water intake should come from the foods we eat, here is a list of foods with high water content: lettuce, watermelon, broccoli, grapefruit, milk, orange juice, carrots, yogurt,

● ● ●

"Tests have shown that diet drinks and sugary beverages alike make us gain weight and are dangerous for our health."

● ● ●

and apples. It is hard to maintain and build endurance without giving your body the tools it needs, so remember to add in these foods and make sure you're drinking enough water. This will help you as you begin training your body to endure everything that life throws your way.

Equally important to physical hydration is the spiritual replenishment promised in Isaiah 58:11. "The LORD will guide you always . . . . You will be like a well-watered garden, like a spring whose waters never fail" (NIV). A well-watered garden is exactly what you'll need to be as you grow in endurance.

Walking with God

There is something uniquely spiritual about taking an early morning walk—enjoying the great outdoors as we commune with God about our day. Walking in the morning, I often sense that it's just me and God, discussing the day ahead. From Psalm 5:3 we learn; "In the morning, O LORD you hear my voice; in the morning I lay my requests before you and wait in expectation" (NIV).

Years ago, I discovered that exercising in the morning awakens and strengthens my body while pouring energy into all of my cells. The first exercise that my cardiologist suggested after surgery was walking. The doctor knew that walking would provide just the right cardiovascular level for my mending heart. The key to rebuilding my endurance was taking it one step at a time—literally, by walking.

Doctors did not originate the idea that walking is beneficial. In Genesis 3, God is walking in the garden in the cool of the evening. As He walks, God wants Adam to commune with Him. So it is that when we walk, we can enjoy the beauty of God's creation and look for Him to commune.

If you would like to combine your physical and spiritual endurance exercises, try walking with God for fifteen minutes each day. You will indeed experience His supernatural strength. Increase your time spent with Him by two minutes per week and the peace that transcends all understanding will embrace you from head to toe.

Regardless of your circumstances or situation, He will see you through—He will help you endure more than anything else on this earth. The benefits of time spent exercising with God are immeasurable. You will start to notice a decrease in your stress and anxiety level, cholesterol, body fat, blood pressure and insulin levels. Most important, our hope and faith increase as we allow God to direct our steps each day.

Allowing God to initiate our steps keeps our minds focused on walking straight ahead as we fix our eyes on Him. The book of Proverbs tells us that all of our ways are in full view of the Lord and that the Lord determines our steps. As you pour out your heart to God while walking, He pours out His blessings of peace and direction.

Here is a prayer that I say out loud each morning while spending time with God. You may find it helpful or you may want to create your own:

"Lord Jesus, I ask that You will direct my steps today. I want to walk and move with You all day long. Protect my steps and direction, Lord, as You lead me. Keep my feet from wandering off Your path today. If I wander off Your path, quickly place me back on the path of righteousness. I desire to walk where You want me to walk today, Lord. Amen."

Once you have taken the first step by consistently walking, you'll find that your endurance will be elevated. Then, you'll be ready to take the next step: running. Remember, no matter how slow or fast you run, God keeps pace with you.

Keep Your Eyes on God's Prize

Running is not something I would recommend to a person just beginning to exercise. Even though I have devoted twenty-five years to training, I did not venture into running until several years into my fitness journey. That's not to say you shouldn't run—it's one of the greatest tests of endurance a person can experience—it's just that you need a good cardiovascular foundation before hitting the pavement. In other words, you can run, but you have to walk first.

The initial step in learning how to train our bodies to run is to become accustomed to the change of pace. When I teach a group of people to run, I start by training them to power walk. Power walking is fast and challenging. If a person can walk briskly for thirty minutes, I know they are ready to progress to a run-walk program.

A run-walk program starts off with a five- to ten-minute easy walk to warm up the body. After the warm-up, you can pick up the pace and run for one minute and then switch to walking for two minutes. Repeat this run-walk pace for up to thirty minutes. Practice that run-walk routine for about two weeks. After two weeks, try alternating two minutes of running with two minutes of walking. By this time you will probably be ready to gradually increase the amount of running and decrease the time walking. Over a six- to eight-week period of time, you'll probably be able to run for fifteen continual minutes and walk for one minute. Within another few weeks, you'll likely run for thirty minutes without walking in between.

It's important to cool your body down after you run by walking for about five to ten minutes to recover and lower your heart rate.

Running is not suitable for everyone. If you have a problematic back or knee injuries, walking or swimming would be more appropriate. But if you are physically able, you'll find that running is challenging but very rewarding. It's an unrivaled cardiovascular exercise that increases lung capacity and strengthens the heart. I have also found that running slims down my hips, legs and thighs. And when I run, I feel empowered and strong.

Once you have conquered running for thirty minutes, three days a week, you may want to consider signing up for a local 5K race and putting your endurance to the test. Competing in a race is something I would suggest that everyone experience. There is something about hundreds of people surrounding you as you run together and compete for a prize. Some people enjoy entering races for the purpose of just finishing the race, while others feed off the competition. I began racing to test my own physical endurance. Instead of competing against someone else, I competed against myself.

But just as in all physical activity, as well as competition, our focus can easily shift. Whose race are we running and why?

After my first race, I continued to run and I got much faster. I ran several more races and placed with impressive speeds. But my racing days came to a screeching halt after about three years. In those days, Robin and I lived in a two-story brick house with a basement. The basement was the kids' domain, sprinkled with their sports memorabilia and trophies lining the walls. My trophies—close to fifty of them—were displayed in a special place in the basement, with their own shelving. When the children's friends would visit, they would comment on the number of first-place trophies that I had won. I would try not to act like it was any big deal and begin to point out the children's trophies. But secretly I would think, "Yes, those are mine. I am some athlete, aren't I?"

One day, I was down in our basement admiring my trophies and I noticed that two of them were broken. It looked like the kids had tried to mend the broken pieces back together and were not very successful. One of the figures was totally decapitated. Finding my prized possessions broken caused me to come unglued. I started yelling and screaming at the children to come down and explain what had happened to my beautiful trophies. "Who broke my trophies? Don't you realize how hard I worked to win these? You kids are disrespectful and rude."

Nobody admitted to anything. To make matters worse, my ten-year-old twin sons started snickering at the sight of the headless trophy. I threatened to ground my boys for life unless they told me the truth. Their innocent Norman Rockwell faces pierced my heart for a brief moment as I stomped up the stairs and made my way to my bedroom, slamming the door behind me.

At that very moment, I heard a soft voice whisper to my heart. "What race are you running?" In a twinkling, I realized I had become self-absorbed with all of these races. Running these races was all about me, and I had taken on the mantra of "look at me" instead of "look at Him." I felt deep remorse for my actions and I thought, "Why am I so upset? Those trophies are just things that collect dust!"

I realized in that moment that I was only racing to prove to others that I was a good athlete. I wanted to seem like I belonged in the elite fitness family. I wanted people to talk about how great they thought I was doing. Flattery pumped me up and kept me at a pace in front of others. I was consumed with the almighty "ME," instead of the Almighty God. I walked down the stairs into the basement, took my sons by their hands, and sat them down beside me on the couch. "Boys, I am so sorry that I yelled at you. Will you forgive me?" We hugged and then the boys looked at each other mischievously. "Sure, Mom. Now can we watch SpongeBob?"

I made a decision right there in the midst of my apology to pack up all of my trophies and put them away. Packing them up was a good purging for my soul. I also decided to stop racing but continue running as a way to keep my cardiovascular endurance level elevated.

Many people still ask me if I will ever race again and I respond, "Maybe one day I will race again, but not until it's God's time."

God teaches us in His Word to run in such a way as to get the prize. Paul tells us in I Corinthians 9 that some people run for a crown that will not last, but we run for a crown that will last forever: "Therefore I do not run like a man running aimlessly; I do not fight like a man beating the air. No, I beat my body and make it my slave so that after I have preached to others, I myself will not be disqualified for the prize" (NIV). God expects each of us to run this race of life with all of our strength, mind, and soul.

If you choose to run, do so because it makes you more able to endure life and because God has given you life.

Shaped by God

Just as cardiovascular exercise is the foundation for physical endurance, spiritual endurance requires a strong foundation. Key elements of that foundation in my life have been daily Bible reading, praying, confessing, exercising and suffering. Without spiritual endurance, our souls weaken and life becomes too hard to handle. Spiritual endurance doesn't make life easy, but it certainly makes life more rewarding and more enjoyable. Getting to the place where we can endure and depend on God every day for everything is powerful.

In order to increase our spiritual endurance, we have to take it one step at a time, just as we do with exercise. Start small, and then keep building until you have a strong spiritual foundation. We do this so that when a trial comes our way, we will be prepared to endure it. I know that had I not built up spiritual endurance, my body might have been able to handle two open-heart surgeries, but I'm not sure my soul would have.

Christians are, of course, not shielded from difficulties or trials. But that's a good thing. Suffering is a key element for gaining spiritual endurance. As we suffer, we are strengthened because our relationship with Christ gains intensity. And suffering not only builds our spiritual endurance, it becomes the true test of it. All of us will experience some sort of exceptionally painful time. It may be the loss of a loved one, an illness or disease, or a hardship of another kind. Whatever pain you go

"In order to increase our spiritual endurance, we have to take it one step at a time, just as we do with exercise. Start small, and then keep building."

through, having spiritual endurance helps you trust that God is right there for you. We are to endure because Christ endured for us.

So what does spiritual endurance training look like? For me, endurance training began by reading the Bible daily. Knowing what the Word says will help you grow stronger. The Word of God is your sword of truth. If you don't already have a Bible reading plan, you might start by reading a chapter of Proverbs every day. By reading a proverb each day, we begin to gain wisdom and knowledge from the written Word of God. Wisdom is a proven principle to gaining spiritual endurance, because by gaining wisdom, we choose God's way instead of our own.

Another important way to improve spiritual endurance is to pray. Training ourselves to pray is quite simple. Don't worry about using eloquent words in your prayer time with God; simply go to your heavenly Father with an open heart, as if talking to a friend. Conversation with God *is* prayer and it is essential for strengthening our souls.

For instance, the more time you spend with a friend, the closer you become to her. The same holds true with God: The more conversations you have with Him, the closer you are to Him. By knowing Him, you soon realize all His power and strength is available simply by asking for His favor. Suddenly life becomes what it was intended to be: you and God on a wonderful journey.

As I continued my spiritual training, I realized that I also needed to find women who had greater spiritual strength than me. I sought out their advice and tried to apply it to my own life. I have not met anyone who has it all down pat, but I have met some wonderful people who have encouraged me and helped me navigate the training ground to

Christian maturity. We all need to help each other on this journey. We gain strength from one another as we run the race together, fixing our eyes on Christ.

Shaped by Prayer

YOU SAVED ME, LORD JESUS, ONCE AGAIN;
YOU SPARED MY LIFE, AND I AM GRATEFUL.
I WILL SHOUT FROM THE ROOFTOPS WHAT YOU
HAVE DONE FOR ME. USE ME AS YOU WILL.
I WILL DO WHATEVER YOU HAVE PLANNED
FOR ME; I AM WILLING AND READY. EQUIP
ME, LORD, WITH ALL THAT I WILL NEED FOR
THE DAYS AHEAD. INCREASE MY FAITH AND
MY PHYSICAL STRENGTH AS I WALK THROUGH
THE DOORS THAT YOU HAVE OPENED FOR ME.
I LOVE YOU, LORD, WITH ALL OF MY HEART,
AND I PRAY THAT MY LIFE PLEASES YOU.
GLORY, GLORY, GLORY TO YOU, O LORD.

Chapter Ten

MAY THE WORDS OF MY MOUTH AND THE
MEDITATION OF MY HEART BE PLEASING IN YOUR
SIGHT, O LORD, MY ROCK AND MY REDEEMER.

PSALM 19:14 (NIV)

Both Robin and I love to work. We thrive on routine and the feeling of accomplishment when a plan comes together. Sometimes in the spring and summer, Robin—who runs an insurance business—will have clients who call in storm claims and, on occasion, they are catastrophic in nature. His normal insurance sales work continues, but on top of that, he may have two or three hundred storm claims to resolve with his clients. Because he is conscientious, the work can be physically and emotionally overwhelming, leaving him drained. Even still, the man is reluctant to rest. He is a workhorse! His idea of a sabbatical is three hours on his lawn mower with no telephone.

Truth be told, I am no better. With seven children in the household, there are always laundry, meals, the children's sports practices, church obligations, and my husband to love and care for. Of course, there is also my work, and it is very important to me. Much of the time, I leave rest for Sunday after church. And maybe, once during the week, I'll stop to have a cup of coffee with a friend. That's it. Otherwise, it's go, go, go.

But even still, I am not as tightly scheduled as I used to be.

Shaped by Life

One Sunday morning as Robin and I were preparing to go to church, he received a shocking phone call. His mentor, Bruce, the man who had invited him into the insurance business, had died of a heart attack. Robin was distraught, and for several weeks, he was changed. He seemed to come to terms with how fragile life was. Bruce was a young, healthy man who did take time to rest, and often encouraged Robin and me to do the same. We were tireless workers, and Bruce used to admonish us about it.

Not long after Bruce's passing, the company Robin represented offered an incentive trip to San Francisco for those with top sales. That's when Robin cooked up a plan: To honor his mentor, Robin told me he was going to win that trip and offer it to me as a real honeymoon. I thought about our first so-called honeymoon, which was really just three days of insurance meetings at a convention. We had enjoyed our time together but vowed that someday we would have a real honeymoon, with "us" being the only real agenda.

I looked at the requirements for winning the trip—it meant extra work, which seemed ironic—and I asked him if it was really a good idea. He looked at me with intensity in his eyes and said that spending a week on vacation with me was worth the initial sacrifice. I got excited, too, at the prospect of a real honeymoon with Robin.

His commitment to meeting the goal was immediate and lasted the whole year. During the tougher times, he would often smile and say to me, "The harder the work, the sweeter the rest." And he was right. After the company announced the winners, Robin and I began to pack for the trip.

As we boarded the huge plane, I began to reflect on the journey that had brought us there: the years of prayer for a good husband, God blessing me with Robin, and the many times we were so exhausted from our busy lives that we could not sleep. I knew that God was providing us with a special time of rest and rejuvenation.

Even the flight was terrific: We had gourmet food, ate ice cream, and watched two wonderful videos. We seldom go to the movies, so to watch two felt luxurious. I would have been happy if the plane had turned around and taken us back home, it had been that enjoyable. But there was more, much more, rest to come.

As we entered the city, we were given a historical tour of the landmarks. Our guide told us we would be staying at the Westin St. Francis on Union Square. He bragged about the hotel, explaining that eighteen presidents, along with countless other dignitaries, had stayed there. After arriving, it was easy to understand why—it was magnificent. It had gourmet restaurants, world-class shopping, a spa and more, all inside the hotel. It even featured a state-of-the-art exercise facility . . . but I never looked in its direction. I was there to rest.

One of our first stops was Chinatown, only a block from our hotel. We'd met another couple, so we walked and talked with them as we shopped. Back home, we seldom go out and socialize, so visiting with other couples was mentally invigorating and enjoyable. Even though I was not exercising intensely, I was still using my muscles by walking around town. Venturing further away from the hotel, we found Fisherman's Wharf, a busy attraction. Our first sighting was sea lions sunbathing on the pier. The sea creatures had completely overrun the area and seemed to enjoy watching the tourists. I remember taking a cue from them: They were able to rest even with constant activity going on around them. Robin and I laughed and laughed when we saw one lion, lying still near the water, serving as a diving board for the other lions. Surely if these animals could rest, I could do the same.

On one of the days, we rented a car with two other couples for a road trip to Muir Woods National Monument. The park is home for the coastal redwoods, the tallest trees in the world. By now, not only were we enjoying each other, we were also becoming more thankful to God for this opportunity. As we stood in the middle of this great forest, we felt shielded from the world. The trees were so tall that the sun was completely hidden from our view. The shade from the trees lowered the temperature in the woods and we began to think we were in another world. For a moment, I just stared at the magnificent creation before me, wondering if it was the way Eden looked before the fall of man. God was giving me a view from a different window and it was breathtaking. I felt as though I was witnessing Genesis 2:2 in person, when God said, "And on the seventh day God ended His work which He had done, and He rested on the seventh day from all His work which He had done" (NKJV). I was experiencing God and learning to rest in His wonderful creation. It was like going to visit God in His neighborhood.

After leaving the park, we decided to take a drive down Highway 1 to enjoy the coast. Several times we stopped to take in the views of the Pacific Ocean. When we arrived at Pebble Beach, the sun was setting as we strolled arm in arm along the beach. We enjoyed a romantic dinner at a little Italian restaurant near the beach, while watching the sun sink into the ocean. It was amazing.

Theresa's Top Three for Rest

1 Nurture your creativity and do whatever it is that brings you pleasure. Is it baking, gardening, working with wood, scrapbooking, sewing, reading or something else?

2 Renew your spirit by making time each day for conversation with God.

3 Schedule rest as well as exercise! I suggest being active five days of the week, if you can, and resting for two.

As we crossed the Golden Gate Bridge back into the city, I felt like I was just moving from one beautiful view to another. It seemed like the lights of the city were dancing on the water as we rolled along the marvelously engineered suspension bridge. And as we laid our heads down on the pillows that evening, after the long day surrounded by God's creation, we knew our sleep would be restful and sweet.

Finally, Robin wanted to see a baseball game while we were in San Francisco. He has always been a baseball fan—his baseball memorabilia decorates the walls in our basement. He actually still collects baseball cards.

After planning the details with the concierge, we headed off for the stadium. Robin became ecstatic when we realized that our seats were right next to the Giants' dugout. We could actually see the sweat on the ballplayers' faces. I couldn't tell you much about the game except that Barry Bonds hit a home run into McCovey Cove, but I can tell you a lot about what I saw in Robin during that game. I watched him take in every play and I saw the little boy in him rise to the surface. The game was full of wonderful, pure moments, as I watched my husband rest as a child of God.

Even though we spent a lot of time with other couples, we had the best time when we were alone together. We became reacquainted and remembered why God had joined us together. Yes, He wanted us to be parents, but He also wanted us to enjoy an intimate husband and wife relationship. He had made us for one another, but life's distractions were keeping us from spending enough time together. We used the quiet time to evaluate our life and to plan adjustments to our schedule so that we could have more time together. Our "real" honeymoon was a wake-up call; it stirred our love for each other and gave us rest, and, in turn, it demanded a reciprocal response from us. We knew we would forever approach the balance of work and rest differently.

Shaped by Fitness

Leonardo da Vinci made an astute observation about five hundred years ago and it still applies today. He said, "Every now and then go away, have a little relaxation, for when you come back to your work your judgment will be surer. Go some distance away, because then, the work appears smaller, and more of it can be taken in at a glance, and a lack of harmony and proportion is more readily seen." I am confident da Vinci was referring to his gift of artistry, but are his words not applicable to us?

Initially, I thought resting on my honeymoon with Robin might be challenging. But once I recognized the importance and value of rest, my outlook changed. Resting, for me, became a time of self-examination and, most important, peaceful healing.

Many folks' work hours have been extended because of advanced technology. In what seems like a lifetime ago, a person used to go home from work and do things to relax. Now, practically every waking moment is spent doing things that keep our bodies busy and minds racing to beat the clock. But experts in the mental health field suggest that to combat mental health issues, it is necessary for the mind to have idle time. Improved mental health relies on our taking time to contemplate, meditate and recharge our minds.

Before antibiotics and vaccines were discovered, the best-known medicine available was rest. Nowadays, even with the glut of medicine we have on the market, researchers still suggest that for healthy individuals to remain healthy, the best preventive medicine is to get more rest. Failing to follow this prescription forces the immune system to become vulnerable to diseases and viruses. In addition to immune system issues, when we don't get enough rest, our ability to concentrate and think clearly is severely impacted. And it is scientifically proven that failing to get enough rest will also increase the possibilities of acquiring the "grumpy syndrome!" Truly, moodiness is just one of many symptoms that could be avoided by creating boundaries between our work and our rest.

• • •

"Before antibiotics and vaccines were discovered, the best-known medicine available was rest. Nowadays, even with the glut of medicine we have on the market, scientists' findings remain the same."

• • •

I have also learned the importance of taking time off to rest my body after working out. For years, I have worked out five days in a row—Monday through Friday—and rested my body on the weekends, spending the time with my family. Those two days without intense exercise allow my body to recover and my muscles to rebuild. As you establish a workout routine, selecting resting days will be important for you too. It doesn't matter how you schedule your time, but I recommend taking two days without exercise during the week, which means that ideally, you will work out five days a week. I know that not everyone is able to devote five days a week to working out—I am fortunate that it's a job requirement for me—but it's best for your body's health and shape if you can. Nonetheless, whether you work out three or five days a week, take the other days to actively rest. What that means is that you're purposeful about resting, both with inactivity and with intentional, recovery-centered movements.

On my recovery days, I often take walks on our farm or do simple Pilates stretches at home, but for the most part, I give my body time off to recuperate. Sometimes I treat myself to a body massage to help my muscles recover more quickly. A body massage helps increase our circulation and releases muscle tension. Besides that, it feels so good!

Stretching on recovery days is a wonderful way to feel rested and help your body stay relaxed. There are so many wonderful stretches you can do to help your body keep moving and be flexible. Here are a few of those stretches that you can do at home.

HIP/GLUTE STRETCH
(RELEASES TIGHT HIP FLEXORS THAT CAUSE PAIN IN THE HIPS, BACK, HAMSTRINGS AND KNEES)

Begin by lying on the floor with both knees bent. Cross your right foot over your left knee. Place your hands behind your left thigh. Exhale and gently pull your leg in toward you while keeping your upper body relaxed. Hold this for 15–30 seconds. Repeat this stretch on the opposite leg.

Hip/Glute Stretch

*Standing Hamstring
Stretch*

STANDING HAMSTRING STRETCH
(RELEASES TIGHT HAMSTRING MUSCLES THAT CAN CAUSE BACK PAIN)

I love to do this stretch while waiting in line at the grocery store. Stand up tall with your abdominals engaged and straighten your left leg on a step or bench. (Or place your foot on the bottom of your grocery cart.) Keep your right knee slightly bent and hold on to a wall (or the cart handle) for support, or place your hands on your hips. Exhale and gently hinge forward at your hips until you feel a mild stretch in the back of your left leg. Keep your spine lengthened and abdominals contracted. Hold for 15–30 seconds. Repeat this stretch on the opposite leg.

Iliotibial Band Stretch

ILIOTIBIAL BAND (ITB) STRETCH
(RELEASES A TIGHT ITB MUSCLE—WHICH RUNS UP YOUR THIGH—THAT MAY CAUSE PAIN IN THE OUTER KNEE OR HIP)

To stretch your ITB, cross your left leg over your right leg at the ankle. Exhale and extend your left arm overhead while reaching toward your right side. Your right hand can rest down your side or on your hip. You should feel this stretch along your left hip. Breathe deeply as you do this stretch and hold for 15–30 seconds. Repeat this stretch on the opposite side.

Customized Rest Programs

Taking rest days is important and so is taking breathers while you exercise. Whether you do weight training, cardio work, Pilates, or all of the above, giving yourself appropriate recovery time is key.

WEIGHT TRAINING

Strength training is an important component to incorporate into our workout routines. The benefits of strength training twice a week will help you lose fat, lower your blood pressure, reduce injury and make you stronger.

If you choose to include all of your muscle groups in one strength session, you could start with the upper body and work your way down, or work the lower body first and work your way up. I prefer to start with the chest and then move to the back, shoulders, triceps, biceps, and abdominal muscles. Then I move on to the lower body with squats and lunges.

When lifting lighter weights with more repetitions (10–15 repetitions) to increase your endurance and lower body fat, you should rest and stretch for thirty seconds to one minute between each set. If you are lifting heavier weights with fewer repetitions (8–12 repetitions) to gain more muscular strength, it usually takes two to five minutes for your muscles to rest before beginning the next set.

If your exercise routine includes weight training, your body will need at least four to eight hours to recover after a strength training session. For this reason, it's important to alternate strength training days by every other day. If you prefer to strength train more often, you should work the upper body one day and the lower body the next or vice versa to avoid working the same muscle groups on consecutive days. Overtraining the muscles by weight lifting on consecutive days will likely damage the muscle and stunt your progression. If you plan recovery days into your week, you will prevent muscle fatigue and injury.

CARDIO

Cardiovascular exercise works differently from strength training, because it aims to build endurance and keep your heart rate strong. For that reason, you should keep up your heart rate for as long as you can without stopping—up to forty-five minutes—during one cardio session. If you are just beginning to do cardio work, start small with five to ten minutes of intensity, followed by two minutes of slowed pace. Then, try to fit in another five to ten minutes, and keep the same pattern for up to forty-five minutes. That pattern is called interval training and is meant to provide rest while still keeping your heart rate elevated.

The American College of Sports Medicine recommends devoting three to five days a week to cardiovascular exercise. Ideally, you should alternate days of intense cardiovascular exercise with a day of rest.

PILATES

If you take Pilates classes, your instructor should automatically provide moments of rest between some of the flow movements and will certainly offer a cooldown at the end of the session. If you are doing Pilates at home, be sure to take at least two or three thirty-second rest periods during your session, and don't skimp on the cooldown. Allowing your muscles and synapses to slowly cool off will be important in your muscles' development.

Restful Activities

Most likely you're reading this book because you know that you don't work out enough, so a chapter on resting from exercise hardly seems necessary for you. I am well aware of that possibility, but I trust that as you move forward on your wellness journey, exercise will become more and more of a habit, and, soon enough, you will find yourself needing more rest than you expected. But one thing we all can relate to is that most of us need recovery from the demands of everyday life. We need to rest our minds, our bodies, and our souls from routine and responsibility. We need rejuvenation.

The experts agree: One of the healthiest ways we can press the reset button, so to speak, is to engage in an alternative activity that we enjoy. Doing something pleasurable—something that makes you, and you alone, feel rested—is proven to provide the *oomph* you need to get through the normal stuff of life. Whether that's baking, working with wood, scrapbooking, painting, gardening, reading . . . if it provides a twinge of happiness, you know you're on the right track. I do, however, recommend veering your rest activities away from technology. Watching TV or surfing the Web may feel relaxing, but it's not active relaxing. It doesn't require you to be creative, it doesn't allow much room for introspection, and it doesn't highlight the wonder of God's beauty. There is a place and time for tele-

● ● ●

"There is a place and time for television and the Internet, but try to spend the majority of your resting time doing something that engages your creative and worshipful energy."

● ● ●

vision and the Internet, but try to spend the majority of your resting time doing something that engages your creative and worshipful energy.

For instance, many people enjoy gardening. When these women start to feel overwhelmed or anxious, they can put on their gardening gloves and experience peace in spirit and body. The meditation of gardening—as you trim, dig, and plant—directs you to God's ability to have a plan for the whole world, yet still create a budding flower, something so small and seemingly insignificant. So, you see, the garden can be a tranquil place to rest and meet one-on-one with God.

Gardening engages muscles similar to those used in cooking/baking, painting, and many other creative activities. In most of those activities, your back and shoulders are energized along with your quadriceps muscles (thighs) and hip flexors. Here are some flexibility exercises you can do before, after, or during your relaxing activities. They are wonderful tools to enhance your relaxation even further.

SPINE ELONGATION STRETCHES

1. Stand up tall and scoop your belly button toward your spine as you walk for five to ten minutes.

2. Stand up tall and exhale as you reach both of your arms overhead toward the sky. Hold for a count of five. Inhale and lower your arms to your sides. Repeat this five times.

BACK STRETCHES

1. Cat Stretch: Begin by positioning yourself on your hands and knees, with your arms and legs comfortably under your shoulders and hips. Keep your abdominal muscles contracted and your spine extended. Exhale and arch your back (cat) and drop your head down, keeping space between your chin and your chest. Hold for a count of five. Inhale and reverse the direction. Hold again for a count of five. Repeat this exercise five times.

2. Child's Pose: Position yourself on your hands and knees and slowly reach your spine back as you extend your arms over your head and rest them on the floor with your palms facing down. Your head should be resting on the floor with your face looking straight down—you may even want to place your forehead on the floor. Exhale and hold this stretch for five counts. Do this exercise at any point when your back feels discomfort.

3. Back Stretch: Lie on your back with your legs extended out and your arms at your sides. Exhale and slowly pull your right knee to your chest (hand positioned behind knee). Hold this for five counts. Inhale and lower your leg back down to the floor. Repeat this exercise with your left leg. Repeat this exercise five times on each leg.

Recovery from Injury or Pain

Sometimes resting is a vacation, while other times it is the result of an injury or illness. Many of my students come to Pilates classes with requests for help to rehabilitate anything from minor to serious injuries. Some have back trouble; some have neck stiffness. Some have knee cricks, and others still, debilitating pain. Pilates is an excellent way to rehabilitate many injuries—although be sure to see your doctor if the pain is intense; you may need a physical therapist.

Pilates exercises will help anyone rehabilitate from head to toe after an injury, surgery, or pregnancy. The Pilates method to fitness is therapeutic and rehabilitative. Since there is great attention to detail in posture and body alignment, it is a perfect way for a person to gain or regain strength in their muscles and joints. Several of my students have fully recovered from back injuries, knee and hip replacements, shoulder, neck and arm pain, and breast cancer surgery by doing Pilates and strength training exercises. All of them started out by modifying the exercises, and, over several weeks, they steadily progressed as their bodies allowed.

"Modifications" is one of the qualities that make Pilates so unique and effective. They allow for injured folks or those with intense muscle tightness to participate in the movements without overexerting their bodies. In modifications, the intention is to gradually intensify the activity until you have been restored to the prior condition, or, of course, have gained deeper flexibility. The length of the rehabilitation process will vary depending on the degree of separation from the prior condition. For instance, a person who hasn't exercised for twenty years and wants to be a marathoner will have a long period of modifications or rehabilitation. On the other hand, a frequent runner with an arm injury may only modify their workout for a few weeks.

When a person combines Pilates and strength training exercises along with healing Scriptures, there is a physical and spiritual healing that takes place in the body that is extraordinary. We can strengthen and heal our bodies when we meditate on things above while exercising in His spirit.

Here are some Pilates and strength training combinations that I recommend for rehabilitating your body. Add the Scriptures to each exercise and you will feel yourself becoming more whole, from the crown of your head to the soles of your feet!

ARM CIRCLE

I will praise you as long as I live, and in your name I will lift up my hands. Psalm 63:4 (NIV)

Lie on the floor supine (face up). Bend both knees, place both feet flat on the floor, and imprint your spine into the mat. Extend your arms straight up and keep your elbows slightly bent. Inhale and circle your arms toward each other five times. Exhale and circle your arms in the opposite direction, still keeping them close to each other, five times. Repeat this exercise five times in each direction.

THE BRIDGE

Let us love one another, for love comes from God. . . . 1 John 4:7 (NIV)

Lie on the floor in a supine (face up) position. Bend both knees and keep your feet flat on the floor as you imprint your spine into the mat. Place your arms at your sides and reach through your fingertips. Inhale and pull your naval to your spine while you begin to roll up into a bridge position, articulating your spine. Exhale and lower down to the vertebra one bone at a time. Repeat this five times.

OPPOSITE ARM AND LEG

I praise you because I am fearfully and wonderfully made. . . . Psalm 139:14 (NIV)

Begin by placing your hands and knees on the floor. Place your hands directly under your shoulders with your knees directly under your hips. Keep your spine and core neutral. Exhale and extend your left arm straight out in front of you and your right leg behind you. Hold this for three seconds. Inhale and lower your arm and leg back to the floor or hover them over the floor. Repeat this ten times. Switch arms and legs and repeat ten times.

SEATED STABILITY BALL CHEST FLY

But those who hope in the LORD will renew their strength. They will soar on wings like eagles; they will run and not grow weary, they will walk and not be faint. Isaiah 40:31 (NIV)

Sit up tall on a stability ball with good posture and one- to three-pound dumbbells (or cans or water bottles) in each hand. With both arms bent ninety degrees, bring your arms in front of your body and elbows close together. Exhale as you bring both arms out to the sides of your body and feel a stretch across the chest. Hold this for three seconds. Inhale and bring the arms back to the front of the body in their starting position. Repeat this exercise 8–12 times for 1–3 sets.

RELAX

"Come to me, all you who are weary and burdened, and I will give you rest. Take my yoke upon you and learn from me, for I am gentle and humble in heart, and you will find rest for your souls. For my yoke is easy and my burden is light." Matthew 11:28–30 (NIV)

Lie on your mat in a supine position with your legs extended out and your arms at your sides. Relax your body and let your head fall to one side and close your eyes. Deeply inhale through your nose and release the tension in your face as you exhale. Inhale and begin to feel the pressure lifting off your shoulders; then exhale slowly. Continue your deep breathing exercise as you relax your body from head to toe and meditate on your relationship with God. Let your mind embrace the Almighty God as He speaks to you.

Friendships and Rest

At the risk of sounding flippant, social interaction can be taxing. We are required, out of respect, to treat people well, even when they treat us quite differently. Often, preserving civility or your own dignity can seem impossible, whether you're dealing with a coworker, teacher, or family member. Some of us may be more interested in retreating from *all* social interaction in order to stay sane. But, even though it may seem counterintuitive, the best way to rest from trying relationships is with a good friend. Letting your hair down with someone you enjoy spending time with restores your faith in relationships and offers a rest from everyday life.

I have always been picky about whom I choose to befriend. I guess this is the reason why I can count my dearest friends on one hand. But I'm picky because I demand a lot of my friends, and I demand a lot of myself as a friend. The greatest demand: Allow me to be myself, to tell the truth, and to vent to you. If a friend is willing to accept that call, she will be one of the greatest sources of rest in your life.

But friendship requires mutual responsibility. To have a good friend, you must be a good friend. The basic ingredient for friendship is unconditional love. In Proverbs 17:17 the Bible says, "A friend loves at all times" (NIV).

I met my closest friend Cindy when I was in my early twenties and we are still close today, even though we live eight hundred miles apart. She is the type of friend who listens and listens without interrupting me. Cindy was there for me during the most difficult times in my life. I can discuss my deepest burdens and concerns with her, and know that our conversation will not be repeated to anyone. She can also tell me her deepest secrets and I keep them close within my heart. She always makes me feel refreshed and encouraged whenever I speak with her.

I'm sure you can relate. For most of us, we can literally feel our muscles ease up after a good girlfriend conversation. The physical benefits of supportive friendships are as profound as any workout we can do and provide us with great opportunities for rest.

● ● ●

"We expect our friends to allow us to be ourselves, to tell the truth and to vent. If a friend is willing to accept that call, she will be one of the greatest sources of rest in your life."

● ● ●

Shaped by God

My grandparents took the Sabbath seriously. They went to church on Sunday morning to worship and rested in the afternoon. After lunch, they would push the screen door open to their porch and spend the afternoon sharing stories with neighbors, family and friends. Everyone had a real life experience to share, and it was carefully expressed to bring encouragement and wisdom to their community. Being still was the only goal on Sunday afternoons and being able to rest was the reward for six days of work. When I think of the Sabbath, I can still hear that ol' screen door creaking.

> "I know in order to fully recover physically, I need to focus my attention on things above. The Word of God says, 'Set your mind on things above, not on earthly things.'"

I become consciously aware of how I spend my time when I force myself to slow down. While resting stretches and enjoyable activities are a must, my time spent with God—particularly on the Sabbath day—is a top priority. I know that in order to fully recover physically, I need to focus my attention on things above. The Word of God speaks about this in Colossians 3:2, "Set your minds on things above, not on earthly things" (NIV).

I take the Sabbath very seriously—especially after learning about rest on my honeymoon—but I also consider meditating on God's Word as an equally important way to rest in God. There are plenty of times during the day to meditate on His Word, but for me, early in the morning (as much as my body protests) is the best time for me to focus.

After I drag myself out of bed, I stand up tall and stretch my arms overhead to praise God for the day. I know that if I start my day thinking about God, my day will be a powerful one. His Word reminds us to meditate on Him in the early morning. "In the morning, O LORD, you hear my voice; in the morning I lay my requests before you and wait in expectation" (Psalm 5:3, NIV).

Each morning as I make my way to the kitchen, I thank God for blessing me with a good husband and seven unique children. I pray and think about my requests as I fill the coffeepot with water and wait for it to finish brewing.

After my coffee is ready, I sit in the study (my friend calls it the watermelon room because of the cheerful colors) with my cup of coffee and my study Bible. I start with a chapter from Psalms and then move on to my next course of wisdom in the book of Proverbs. God's words seem to leap off the pages and burrow deep into my heart as I read and meditate on what He has to say. I draw close to Him and He draws closer to me.

I cherish these quiet, meditative moments alone with my Father. By reading the Word, I know that the words of my mouth and the meditation of my heart need to be pleasing to God. Whenever you feel low or down, you can depend on God's Word to pick you up. Turn His pages and be filled with His wisdom and love.

I have found the morning to be my best time with God, but it doesn't necessarily have to be scheduled or even quiet. Some of my fondest memories of conversations with God took place in the hectic craziness of raising four children as a single parent. Sometimes I would reprimand my children in one breath, and then walk into the kitchen to fix them dinner and praise God in the next. Seasons are different in everyone's life, so take your season and be creative, making sure that God has a front-row seat in your life. Rest in God as you go about your day and follow in the way that He leads you.

Shaped by Prayer

I AM RESTING IN YOUR ARMS, LORD JESUS.
YOU ARE MY SHIELD AND PROTECTOR. ONLY
YOU KNOW THE OUTCOME OF MY LIFE.
PLEASE FORGIVE ME FOR THE TIMES WHEN I
HAVE NOT BEEN OBEDIENT TO YOU. I KNOW
THAT YOU FORGIVE ME BECAUSE YOU SEE MY
HEART. MAY MY HEART AND SOUL ALWAYS
FIND REST IN YOU. RESTORE MY BODY AND
SOUL AS I CONTINUE DOING THE WORK YOU
HAVE PLANNED FOR ME. THOUGH MY BODY
IS SOMETIMES WEAK, I CAN CALL ON YOU
ANYTIME TO REFRESH ME. EVERYTHING
AROUND ME IS HECTIC, BUT WITH YOU, THERE
IS JOY AND PEACE. I THANK YOU FOR THE
PEACE THAT COMES ONLY FROM KNOWING
YOU. MAY OTHERS GET TO EXPERIENCE YOUR
PEACE IN THEIR LIVES. I AM RESTING IN YOU,
O LORD, MY SAVIOR AND DELIVERER.

A Cooldown

It is not a coincidence that you have read (and completed!) *Shaped by Faith*. God has purpose in all things, after all, and I know He had you in mind when He helped me write this book. I have prayerfully written each page, knowing that it is more than just a prescription for good health or a nice figure, but that God had a greater purpose. I believe that He wants you to pursue whole-person wellness. Thus, my prayer for you is that you begin this journey with joy, patience, and commitment. And I have prayed words of thanks for you and for the gift I was given in creating this book. I am humbled by the process and can thank no one before God.

Truth be told, my thankfulness will only multiply when you choose to apply the lessons in this book to your life. As I said from the outset, these lessons can take a lifetime to learn. I am, after all, asking you to apply not only challenging physical lessons but also spiritual ones. But the trajectory of my own life has made me convinced that neither physical health nor spiritual health can be achieved quite as purely without the fusion of the two.

My life experiences, revealed in this book, were written not only to demonstrate how physicality and spirituality go hand in hand, but also to encourage and inspire those of you who have had similar difficulties or challenging circumstances—in other words, all of you. We all have endured hard times, challenging trials, and flat-out pain. But as I've said several times in this book, those are the moments when we learn and grow the most. So as you go along this journey, pay attention to the trials you face and I'm willing to bet you'll learn a lot of the same lessons I did. God is so faithful that way—He makes sure we know that we are not alone.

Your story, like mine, has been writing itself since birth. But with this book, your whole-person wellness journey has just begun. Even though the opening chapters of your life cannot be rewritten, they can be used to bring spiritual clarity to future chapters. Whether you are eighteen, forty or eighty-seven, whole-person wellness welcomes new story writers all along the way—the more the merrier. Just as I hope my stories have brought hope and encouragement to you, the stories you write along your journey will be used to help others reach happy beginnings, too.

To set you off on this journey, the *Shaped by Faith* DVD attached to this book is a terrific resource. The thirty-minute DVD offers a wellspring of vital exercises that challenge the body and encourage the soul with prayerfully considered Scriptures to accompany each exercise. Both the exercise novice and the pro can experience a wonderful, spiritual workout with this DVD.

And for those of you who like to have a plan, I've included a twelve-month sample schedule to help you implement the many stretches, exercises, and other practices found in this book.

Another resource I hope you take advantage of is my Web site: www.shapedbyfaith.com. This site has many helpful ideas and articles, as well as contact information so you can write me and tell me about your journey. Please feel free to send me comments, stories or questions; I'll do my best to answer you. But most important, God is at your side and available anytime.

It's up to you now to gather your story, your hopes, your fears and your commitment, and take the first step. It will be a long, but joyous and fruitful journey. May God bless and keep you, dear friends.

IN CHRIST,
THERESA

Putting It into Practice

Here is a month-by-month plan to help you slowly begin to implement the things we've talked about in this book. Remember, whole-person wellness isn't just about fitness. Look for ways to incorporate your relationship with God into your stretches and exercises, and find time during the day to pray and read the Word.

Month 1

Start your first month on this journey just becoming aware of your body (see chapter 1). Pay attention to your body and journal what you hear it say. Then begin practicing the breathing exercises in chapter 2.

Bring attention to your posture as you practice standing or sitting tall and scooping your belly (see chapter 5).

If you are feeling particularly motivated, begin your cardiovascular workouts once or twice a week in twenty-minute sessions. Choose a cardiovascular activity that you enjoy and don't stress out about the amount of time you spend working out.

Month 2

Commit to doing cardiovascular exercise twice a week this month to begin building endurance. Write down the days you plan to exercise in your fitness journal or mark them on your calendar. You may want to find an exercise partner and plan your workout days together to stay motivated and committed to exercising (see chapter 3).

Remember to pay close attention to your breathing and posture as you walk together for twenty minutes. If you cannot find a workout partner, take your pet or small child for a walk in the park or in your neighborhood. Scoop your belly and enjoy the day!

Month 3

You should be feeling more motivated and energized this month—you are doing great; Keep going!

Commit to adding a few strength-training exercises to your exercise plan one day a week. You can choose to strength train right after your cardiovascular workout or on a separate day (see chapter 6). Posture and body alignment are important to maintain while you are strength training (see chapter 5).

Continue to pay close attention to how your body is responding to exercise. You should begin to sleep better at night from doing cardiovascular exercise two days a week and by adding a little strength training once a week into your routine.

Scoop your belly and breathe!

Month 4

Was I right—are you getting sounder sleep at night?

This month, carry a water bottle with you wherever you go. Water is your drink of choice, and it will help cleanse your body of deadly toxins. Also, it helps with weight loss and makes you feel better.

Are you ready to increase your cardiovascular exercise? If not, don't worry about it; just continue doing cardio two days a week. If you are up for the challenge, plan on adding one more day of cardiovascular exercise to your week. Remember, you just have to workout for twenty minutes. You can do it! Maybe you'd like to try my Cardio Soul workout to add some diversity to your exercises (see chapter 9).

Continue strength training one day a week. How do you think you are progressing? Take time to write about your progress in your journal or talk about it with your workout partner.

Month 5

Continue taking your water bottle with you everywhere, even shopping!

This month, consider spicing up your cardiovascular exercise by joining a fitness class at a local gym. Your endurance should be higher so I know you can handle a group class. It might be more comfortable if you and your workout partner attend the class together. I remember being intimidated during my first fitness classes because I was out of my comfort zone, but it won't take long until you feel right at home.

Continue doing cardiovascular exercise three times a week and strength training once a week. If you attend a group fitness class once a week, this will count as one day of cardio.

Pay attention to your posture; you should feel taller!

Month 6

I know you are working hard and I appreciate your effort! Doesn't it feel good to know that you are getting stronger each day?

Since you are six months into your workout plan, it's time to work on your core (abdominal and back muscles). Scooping your belly should have strengthened your core and back, so you're ready to grow stronger in that area. Add a few core exercises into your strength-training day (see chapter 7). This should make you feel a little sore!

Continue doing cardiovascular exercise three days a week for twenty minutes. Drink water, breathe, and scoop your belly!

Month 7

Even though I don't know you, I want you to know that I mean it when I say that I'm proud of you. Sticking with a program this long tells me that your mind-set has been going through a total transformation, along with your body.

This month, I am going to ask you to step it up a little in your cardio plan and increase your cardio time to twenty-five minutes. Adding five minutes to each cardio day isn't too hard, and your body is ready for it. Remember, you can walk, take a fitness class, or do anything that keeps your heart rate elevated for twenty-five minutes (see chapter 9). Turning your home into a workout center could make it easier for you to take a little more time with the exercises (see chapter 6).

Continue with your strength training and core exercises one day a week. Drink plenty of water, scoop, and breathe!

Month 8

Keep going strong; you are doing so beautifully!

Continue doing cardiovascular exercise three times a week for twenty-five minutes per session, and strength and core exercises one day a week.

It is now time to incorporate more stretches and Pilates exercises into your fitness plan. Do these when time allows. You can do these at work during a break or in the evenings after dinner; you choose the time and place (see chapter 4).

Breathe easy, drink plenty of water and scoop it!

Month 9

Do you feel like you are ready to birth a completely new body? You have worked so hard that I think you should treat yourself to a new outfit or a body massage this month. You truly deserve it!

Continue doing cardiovascular exercise three times a week for twenty-five minutes, and this month, add another strength-training day. Remember, you can strength train on the same day as you do cardio. Just make sure you strength train on alternating days, or alternate upper and lower body exercises if you need to do consecutive days.

I bet you could do the belly scoop in your sleep by now! Continue your deep breathing exercises and get plenty of water!

Month 10

How does your new outfit look? I imagine that everyone you know is noticing a remarkable change in your attitude and your physical body.

This month you are going to stay steady. Continue doing cardiovascular exercise three times a week for twenty-five minutes. You may want to mix up your cardio plan for variety (see Appendix C for cross training ideas).

Continue strength training twice a week, and remember to stretch afterward (see chapter 4). Include core and back exercises in your strength-training routine.

Your lower back is thanking you for all that belly scooping! By now you should be craving water all the time and getting plenty of restful sleep.

Month 11

You are doing better than good, so keep it up!

It is so important to stay focused in this month. Continue with three days of cardiovascular exercise for twenty-five minutes, and strength train twice a week on alternating days. Drink plenty of water!

Work on your flexibility by incorporating more Pilates exercises into your workout. It might be easy for you to use my *Shaped by Faith* DVD once a week, which is included in this book. This will count as your core and back workout, along with stretching.

You should be standing taller and breathing easy while scooping your belly!

Month 12

I am so proud of you for committing to and continuing on this journey of whole-person wellness. But it doesn't end here: Keep paying attention to how your body is feeling, moving and breathing.

If you feel up to it, increase your cardio time to thirty minutes three days a week, and continue strength training two days a week on alternating days. If you aren't running yet, you might want to give that a try. It will definitely challenge your new body and help you down the road to endurance (see chapter 9).

Increase your flexibility even more by working out to my *Shaped by Faith* DVD twice a week. Don't forget, this video counts as a core and back workout. It also incorporates all the stretches you will need to become elastic.

Scoop, breathe, drink water, and enjoy your newly transformed body!

Nutrition Tips

We are fueled by the foods we eat, so without good nutrition, our wellness journeys will be stunted. But good nutrition is not the same thing as dieting —it only complicates matters when we bounce from one diet to the next. Rather than starving yourself or clinging to some fad diet, why not just learn to eat foods that are good for you? Of course, we all like the occasional treat and you should not swear off indulgences. But as a general rule, making smart choices is the best path you could choose for your body.

What does a healthy diet include?

- Carbohydrates should make up 45–65 percent of our daily intake. Healthy carbohydrate food choices are: whole grains, fruits, vegetables, legumes, pasta, and rice.

- Proteins should make up 10–35 percent of our daily food intake. Proteins are essential to the building, maintenance, and repair of body tissue such as the skin, internal organs, and our muscles. The best foods to choose in this food group are: fish, lean meats, poultry, dairy, eggs, and beans. Women need forty-five grams of protein each day and men need fifty-five grams per day.

• Fats should make up twenty percent of our diet. Fat is made up of compounds called fatty acids and lipids. It's important to eat good fats, such as those found in dairy products, nuts, and oils.

Some basic tips for good nutrition

• Foods that are still in their original state—shape, chemical makeup, etc.—are best. Foods that are processed, battered, deep-fried, coated with sugar, etc., will only drag you down and make you feel uncomfortable for the rest of the day.

• Steamed vegetables like broccoli, green beans, and squash are a delicious way to eat healthily.

• Eating fresh fruits five times a day will curb hunger and keep you going strong. Eating an apple or two a day will supply you with all of the fiber you need, and perk up your metabolism. Replacing white bread and refined pasta with whole grain breads and pastas also makes a dramatic difference in your body's mechanism.

• Preparing foods by cooking with canola and olive oil is a healthy choice—much healthier than cooking with butter.

Foods prepared this way are low in saturated fat, high in antioxidants, and they contain a significant amount of omega-3 fatty acids.

- Did you know that eating fish twice a week keeps your heart healthy? Fish is packed full of omega-3 fatty acids that help us fight off heart disease. I choose to eat fish for my heart and to reduce inflammation in my body. I can always tell when I have eaten fish because my body feels less bloated and my joints function better.

- If you can, try to eat five to six small food items throughout the day. These foods can include a handful of almonds, a piece of fruit, yogurt, a slice of whole wheat bread with turkey, a garden salad or organic peanut butter on celery. Studies have proven that eating five to six small meals during the day will help increase our metabolic rate and fuel our bodies more efficiently.

Of course, you can't expect to completely change your diet immediately. But if you take on these tips one at a time, gradually you will begin to feel healthier. That doesn't mean snack food is never okay. I'm tempted most by sweets. They taste so good going down, but often I feel awful about an hour later. I have discovered that eating fresh fruits, berries, and honey helps to satisfy my sweet tooth. All of us have food weaknesses, but making healthy choices will improve our mood, help us to keep a healthy weight, slow down the aging process, and increase our energy and stamina.

Cross Training Routines

Do you ever get tired of doing the same exercise routine each week? Perhaps you continue to do the same routine out of convenience or maybe you just don't know what else to do. I have a solution for you. Cross training is a perfect match for anyone who is bored in her exercise routine and looking to get beyond a fitness plateau. If your weight and body fat are not improving, you'll know it's time to think outside of the box and find some unique forms of exercise to rev up your metabolism and refuel your tank.

You may think that you are in good shape, but try something different like skiing or mountain biking . . . and you will suddenly feel like a novice. That's a good thing! Cross training keeps your fitness level growing instead of being stagnant.

Cross training also reduces the risk of injury from overusing key muscles and allows you to work the cardiovascular system in a variety of ways that will keep you motivated and moving forward.

Here is a list of cross training exercises you can choose from.

- running
- cycling
- swimming
- jump roping
- stair climbing
- rowing
- skiing (snow boarding)
- hiking
- skating (in-line or ice)
- racquetball/basketball/other court sports
- aerobics
- step aerobics
- strength training (free weights, machines, tubing, bands, body weight exercises)
- flexibility training (Pilates)
- speed and agility drills
- balance drills
- circuit training, sprinting, plyometrics

I like to cross train by doing different forms of cardiovascular training while combining strength training and flexibility exercises, all at the same time. You might recognize some of these from the chapters you've read!

Here are some of my favorite cardiovascular exercises that I mix and match:

- jumping rope, step aerobics, running, power walking, bouncing on the ball, jumping jacks on the ball, skipping, dribbling a basketball or stability ball while jogging, lateral shuffles across the floor, kick boxing and plyometric moves on the step and on the floor

Here are some of my favorite strength-training exercises that I mix and match:

- walking lunges with biceps curls, squats with shoulder presses, reverse lunges and front raises, triceps extensions with tubing, triceps dips off ball, triceps kickbacks with dumbbells, biceps curls standing on one leg, biceps with tubing, upright rows with plié squats, one legged dead lifts, step ups holding weights, and core work on the ball and floor, using weighted ball, stability ball and weighted bar

My flexibility training exercises that I mix and match look like this:

- Pilates mat exercises, stretch band exercises for the upper and lower body, stability ball exercises, and standing stretches for the upper and lower body

Heart Health Information

Exercising has taught me the importance of noticing how my body is feeling at all times. I have become so in tune with my body's mechanics that I know quickly when I have a problem. It's important for you to develop this kind of attention to your body, too, especially when it comes to your heart. Heart disease is one of the most common killers in America and it's something we shouldn't take lightly.

Here are a few heart facts to keep in mind:

- One in three women dies of heart disease each year, making it the number one killer.

- Even though cardiovascular disease accounts for forty-three percent of all female deaths, few women view it as a significant health risk.

- Women who experience frequent symptoms related to heart disease may receive inadequate attention from health care providers compared to men because heart attack symptoms are different for women. So be persistent about getting the help you need.

- Each year, about 88,000 women ages 45–64, and about 372,000 women ages sixty-five and older, have a heart attack.

Factors that increase risk for heart disease:

- Smoking—About 21.2 million women smoke.

- High blood pressure—thirty-three percent of women have hypertension, which affects about 2.5 million women.

- Overweight/Obese—sixty-two percent of women are overweight, including those who are obese.

- Physical inactivity—More women than men are physically inactive, with forty-one percent of women engaging in no leisure physical activity and more than sixty percent not meeting the recommended amount of at least thirty minutes a day of moderate physical activity such as walking.

- Diabetes—Nearly seven million women have been diagnosed with diabetes and another three million are undiagnosed.

Tips for your heart's health:
- Stay physically active.

- Stop smoking and avoid other people's smoke if possible.

- Control high blood pressure and high blood cholesterol through exercise and diet.

- Cut down on fats, saturated fats, and salt in your diet.

- Make a commitment to reduce your weight if you are overweight.

Choose the following cardiovascular activities to keep your heart healthy:
- a brisk walk outside or inside a shopping mall with a friend

- take your pet for a walk

- garden

- swim

- bike

- join a group exercise class

- walk on a treadmill or elliptical trainer

- jog or run

Exercises for Seniors

Research has proven that exercise is safe for people of all ages and that it is one of the healthiest things you can do for yourself, even as an older adult. By staying physically active, you will feel better every day. With exercise, you will prevent many diseases and illnesses that often occur with age such as diabetes, heart disease, osteoporosis, obesity, and certain cancers. If you have not been very active up to now, start off with a small amount of exercise each day by doing gentle movements to keep your joints flexible. Some exercise is far better than no exercise. Healthy aging and independent living is dependent on daily physical activity.

With normal aging, there is a general reduction in muscle mass that occurs in adults. Adults in the fourth decade of life lose 3–5 percent of muscle mass, and the decline increases after the age of fifty. The good news is that we can increase our muscle mass at any age and improvement is noticed almost immediately. Our muscles keep us strong and they help us to burn calories, maintain our weight and contribute to bone strength and balance. But if we do not exercise, our muscles become weak and eventually we will not be able to live independently. Balance also decreases as we age, and according to the U.S. Center for Disease Control and Prevention, one in every three Americans over the age of sixty-five falls each year. And among individuals 65–84, falls account for eighty-seven percent of all fractures and are the second leading cause of spinal cord and brain injury. You can do something to prevent injury and illness: You can exercise.

There are four types of exercises that are essential for older adults: endurance exercises, balance exercise, strength training, and stretching exercises.

If you have not exercised for some time, remember to start out easy, with just five to ten minutes of exercise. Increase your time as your strength increases.

Endurance activities for older adults (cardiovascular)

- walking briskly in a park, on an indoor track or in a mall
- swimming or taking a water aerobics class with a friend
- gardening, mowing or raking the lawn
- bicycling on a stationary bike or outdoors on a level surface with a friend
- dancing
- group fitness classes

Seated Strength-Training Workout for Older Adults (strength and balance)

Seated Shoulder Press on Stability Ball

SEATED SHOULDER PRESS ON STABILITY BALL

Sit on a stability ball with your feet on the floor hip width apart. Keep your spine lifted tall and your abdominals pulled in. Hold each weight or soup can at shoulder height next to your shoulder with your palms facing forward. Exhale and lift the weights over your head slightly in front of your body. Inhale and lower the weights slowly back down to the shoulders. Repeat this exercise 8–12 times for 1–3 sets.

Seated Lateral Arm Raise

SEATED LATERAL ARM RAISE

Sit on a stability ball holding light weights or soup cans in both of your hands with your arms at your sides. Feet should be shoulder width apart and your spine should be tall with your abdominals pulled in. Exhale and lift your arms up to the sides only to shoulder level with your palms facing the floor. Inhale and lower your arms back down to your sides. Repeat this 8–12 times for 1–3 sets.

Seated Triceps Extension

SEATED TRICEPS EXTENSION

Begin by sitting on a ball while holding a medium weight at each end with your hands. Maintain a tall spine and engage your abdominals. Take the weight straight up overhead with your arms next to your ears. Inhale and lower the weight behind your head until your elbows are at ninety degrees. Exhale and squeeze your triceps to straighten your arms without locking them. Repeat for 1–3 sets of 8–12 repetitions.

SEATED BICEPS CURL

Sit up tall with your abdominals engaged while holding both weights in your hands with palms facing out and elbows next to your sides. Exhale and curl the weights up toward your shoulders and squeeze your biceps. Inhale and lower back down to the starting position, keeping a slight bend in your elbows. Repeat for 1–3 of 8–12 repetitions. (You can challenge your balance and core muscles by lifting one foot off the floor during this exercise. Make sure you switch feet on the next set.)

SEATED LEG EXTENSION

Begin by sitting up tall with a scooped belly and both feet flat on the floor hip width apart. You can hold onto the ball on the sides to help with balance. Straighten your right leg out in front of you and flex your foot. Exhale and lift your leg straight up and hold. Inhale and lower your right leg down just above the floor. Repeat this for 10–16 repetitions and then switch to your left leg. Repeat the entire exercise for 1–3 sets on each leg.

Seated Leg Extension

SEATED ROTATION FOR ABDOMINALS

Sit up tall with your belly scooped in holding a light weight or small weighted ball in front of you. Both elbows should be bent and close to your sides. Exhale and rotate the ball to the right while keeping your hips and legs facing forward. Inhale and bring the ball back to the front. Repeat this on the left side. Continue alternating from side to side going slowly as you concentrate on contracting your abdominal muscles. Repeat this exercise on each side 8–12 times for 1–3 sets.

Post-strength-training exercises (flexibility)

BACK STRETCH

Stand or sit up tall and clasp your hands together in front of you with your palms facing away. With your abdominals contracted, exhale and round your back, pressing your arms away from your body. You should feel this stretch in your upper back. Hold this stretch for fifteen seconds and then return to your starting position. Repeat this stretch five times.

SIDE STRETCH ON BALL

Sit up tall with your abdominals contracted. Place your right hand on the side of the ball. Exhale as you lift your left arm overhead and lean to the right. Hold this stretch for fifteen seconds. Inhale and lower your left arm back to your side. Repeat on this side five times and then switch to the other arm.

TRICEPS STRETCH

Stand or sit up tall with abdominals engaged. Exhale and bend your left elbow behind your head and use your right hand to gently pull your left elbow in further. Hold this stretch for fifteen seconds as you feel mild tension in the back of your arm. Switch arms and repeat five times on each arm.